The Collector's

Encyclopedia Of

GLASS CANDLESTICKS

by

Margaret and Douglas Archer

COLLECTOR BOOKS

A Division of Schroeder Publishing Co., Inc.

P.O. BOX 3009 • PADUCAH, KENTUCKY 42001

Photography
by
BRUCE H. LINKER
St. Louis, Mo.

Additional copies of this book may be ordered from:

COLLECTORS BOOKS
P.O. Box 3009
Paducah, Kentucky 42001

or

Mr. & Mrs. Douglas Archer
P.O. Box 919
Kernersville, N.C. 27284-0919

@$19.95 Add $1.00 for postage and handling.

Copyright: Bill Schroeder, Douglas Archer, 1983
ISBN: 0-89145-210-9

WE DEDICATE THIS BOOK TO

STAN & ELEANOR ROSENBLUM

Through the years friendships develop in strange ways; our friendship with Eleanor & Stan developed around the collecting of glass. We have found many friends by this route, but there comes a time when you wish to do something special and/or try to find a way to say "thank you" for the association, generosity, love, and encouragement which these friends have extended to us. We thank you Stan & Eleanor, and dedicate this labor of love to you.

FOREWORD

When we were asked by Collectors Book to create an *Encyclopedia of Glass Candlesticks,* we had some reservation as to our ability to assemble and catagorize enough material to be classified as an encyclopedia (encyclopedia: giving of information on all branches of, and/or one field of knowledge).

We do not profess to have the knowledge of all of the information presented in this publication. Much of it took many years of research and hard work by a lot of generous people who have so unselfishly helped us. Their expertise is the real back-bone of this encyclopedia and we hope that they are not disappointed with our effort, and that we have conveyed the information presented correctly.

We have combined a lot of the items shown in *Glass Candlesticks Books 1 & 2,* and what would have been book 3; expanded it, added as many of sales catalogs as we had access to, to bring to you as much depth on each candlestick as we could find. Unfortunately, we were forced to delete some of the glass houses that appeared in our other books. This was necessary because of space and limited information on those particular glass houses.

We encourage you to read the acknowledgements and reference publications, for these are the people and tools that make this book possible.

Margaret & Douglas Archer

ACKNOWLEDGMENTS

We wish to acknowledge all of the people who helped us with *Glass Candlesticks Books 1 & 2,* for without their help, this publication would not have been possible:

Book 1

Harold Bennett, Cambridge, Ohio
Victor Buck, Upland, California
Nealy Cardwell, Greensboro, North Carolina
Dr. Wilfred Cohen & Dollie, Costa Mesa, California
John D. Hartzog, Titusville, Florida
John D. Hartzog, Jr., Titusville, Florida
Lucile J. Kennedy, Bellaire, Ohio
Ralph & Mildred Lechner, Richmond, Virginia
Everett R. Miller, Rives Junction, Michigan
Eleanor Rosenblum, St. Louis, Missouri
Barbara Shaeffer, Costa Mesa, California
Chris Shields, Huntington Beach, California
Wilma Shouse, Kernersville, North Carolina
Helen Warner, Williamstown, West Virginia
Sherry Woodington, Orange, California

Book 2

Carlton Brown, Dearborn, Michigan
Hugh A. Buzzard, Moundsville, West Virginia
David B. Dalzell, Jr. Moundsville, West Virginia
Frank Fenton, Williamstown, West Virginia
Paul E. Kasler, Columbus, Ohio
Lucile J. Kennedy, Bellaire, Ohio
Nancy O. Merrill, Sandwich, Massachusetts
Jeanne McCormick, Columbus, Ohio
Glenna & Arnold Preheim, Anaheim, California
Eleanor Rosenblum, St. Louis, Missouri
Bill Schroeder, Paducah, Kentucky

In addition to those listed above, there are those who were directly involved and/or helped with this manuscript (involved means: supplied material and/or information, assisted with the indentification of candlesticks, advised, consulted, loaned glass for photographing, and/or reviewed and edited various sections of our work).

WE THANK YOU

Fred Bickenheuser, Grove City, Ohio, for assistance, advice and supplying catalog material to support the Duncan-Miller and U.S. Glass sections.

Hugh A. Buzzard, Moundsville, Ohio, for assistance and glass in the Fostoria section

Ann Chisholm, Kirkwood, Missouri, for loaning us glass (U.S. glass flower floater)

Frank Fenton, Williamstown, West Virginia, for assistance and for taking an interest in the publication in its early stages

Gateway Depressioneers Glass Club of Greater St. Louis

for use of material from their library

Mr. & Mrs. Bill Gentry, Overland, Missouri, for loaning us old magazines with glass advertisements

Mrs. D. Harris, Moundsville, West Virginia, for considerations and assistance with Fostoria shelf signs.

Heisey Collectors of America, Inc. & Louise Ream, Newark, Ohio, for assistance and allowing us to reprint information on Heisey Glass from the *Heisey News* official publication of the Heisey Collectors of America

Acknowledgements (continued)

Kip Hoffman, Ballwin, Missouri, for the loan of Imperial Glass.

Lucile J. Kennedy, Bellaire, Ohio, for again allowing us access to the Imperial Glass Company Archives where we were able, with her kind assistance, to gather much of the material on Imperial, Heisey, and Cambridge Glass. Most of the catalog material for these companies shown came from the Archives at Imperial (the exception being the material supplied by the Heisey Collectors of America). It is amazing how many books would never have been printed without Lucile's help. A very special "thanks" to this lovely lady.

Gail Krouse, Washington, Pa., for assistance and advice on Duncan-Miller.

Mike Lloyd, Ferguson, Missouri, for loaning us glass to photograph. (Duncan-Miller Candelabrum)

Jack Metcalf, Newark, Ohio, for assistance and advice on Heisey.

Don & Jane Rogers, O'Fallon, Missouri, for furnishing us with catalog material, assistance, advice, reviewing the Cambridge section, and loaning us much of the Cambridge Glass shown. And a special thanks to Don who spent many hours (days) helping us with the set-ups during the long photographic sessions. We will miss them, now that we live in North Carolina!

E. Ward Russel, Silver Spring, Maryland, for assistance, advice, and the loan of Imperial and Northwood Glass.

Bill Schroeder, Paducah, Kentucky, for allowing us to use material that appears in other Collector Books publications, and for having faith in us to compile this encyclopedia.

Barbara Shaeffer, Marietta, Ohio, for assistance, advice, research, and for giving us permission to use material from the *Glass Review* Publications.

Wilma A. Shouse, Kernersville, North Carolina and Coos Bay, Oregon, for gramatical assistance and editorial advice.

Bill & Phillis Smith, Cambridge, Ohio, for advice, assistance, and sharing material on Cambridge Glass.

Pat & Dick Spencer, O'Fallon, Illinois, for furnishing us with catalog material, assistance, advice, reviewing the Heisey section, and loaning us much of the Heisey Glass shown. Pat & Dick furnished us with most of the old magazine advertisements shown. We spent many nights at their house going through stacks of material and magazines. To know them is to love them.

Mrs. Paul Teeter, Ballwin, Missouri, for loaning us glass to photograph. (Fostoria Coin Glass).

Berry Wiggins, Orange, Virginia, for assistance and advice on Imperial, Northwood, and other glass.

Mrs. John Wiggins (Pattie), Ballwin, Missouri, for the use of a lot of glass and most of all, for just being a good friend.

Kitty & Russell Umbraco, Richmond, California, for assistance, advice, research, and for giving us permission to use material from their publications.

Roserita Ziegler, New Britain, Connecticut, for advice, assistance, and the loan of Fostoria Glass.

A Special Thanks!

We are very fortunate to be able to present catalog composites of some of the Duncan-Miller 1920's thru 1930's sales catalogs. In addition, we have an unbelievable treat for you in being able to present a number of Duncan-Miller original advertising mats. The advertising mats were reproduced from the originals that were still in the Duncan-Miller Art Department's folders. All the composite materials and photo mats were loaned to us by Mr. Fred Bickenheuser *(Tiffin Glassmasters, Book 1 & 2)*. Fred also furnished the catalogs & catalog materials used in the U.S. Glass section.

Other Duncan-Miller catalog material was furnished by Pat & Dick Spencer of O'Fallon, Ill. This type information is a most valuable asset to the collector and we are very grateful for the privilege to be allowed to present it.

TABLE OF CONTENTS

Boston & Sandwich
1826-1888

1,2,4,5. Dolphins, circa 1830-1888

1. Single step base Circa 1830-1888, clambroth, current value $175.00 - 225.00

2. Single step base Circa 1830-1840, clambroth Dolphin - translucent blue socket. Current value, $225.00 - 275.00

4. Double step base Circa 1850-1888, clambroth Dolphin - translucent blue socket. Current value, $225.00 - 275.00

A step and one-half base (Dolphin) can be found with an acanthus leaf translucent blue socket. The acanthus leaf socket is much larger than the socket on Item 3. A reproduction of the basic candlestick issued by Imperial for the Metropolitan Museum of Art is shown on Plate 35, Item 2&3. Other known colors not shown are canary yellow, crystal, translucent blue, electric blue, opaque jade green (rare). Some double steps were also decorated with gold. The rarest of Sandwich Dolphins is a 8½″ high square-single base. The socket has small Dolphins and sea shells impressed on it. The socket seems a little over-sized for the Dolphin; this is the key for identifying it. (Sorry we did not have one to show you).

5. Reproduction circa 1981

This item is mold-marked and has a paper label from the Colonial Glass Company (made in Taiwan). Also attached is a pamphlet which describes the history of Sandwich Glass. The product is sold by the Colonial Candle of Cape Cod. Color: electric blue. Current value, $18.00 - 25.00

3. Acanthus Leaf, circa 1840-1850, 10¾″ high (also made 9″ high).
Base: opaque white. Applied socket: translucent blue. Also known as Acanthus Scroll. Other known colors: clambroth base - translucent blue socket, opaque base - translucent green socket (very rare color). Current value, $400.00 - 500.00

*The Sandwich Museum Staff Members refer to white glass manufactured at "Boston and Sandwich Glass Company" as "opalescent". It is well to note that reference to this type glass is made as "opaque white" in some publications.

6. Dolphin, circa 1840-1850, 6½″ high.
This candlestick is shown with the Sandwich Glass as we have found reference that it is a Sandwich Candlestick. However, further research indicates that it is not a Sandwich Dolphin, but was made by McKee Brothers of Pittsburgh in the late 1850's. The reference also indicates that it may be found in such colors as vaseline & light peacock blue. We have seen a translucent white base blue socket, and a totally translucent candlestick. Some years ago, the price was $250.00 - $400.00 each. Current value, $75.00 - 100.00.

7. Petal and Loop, circa 1835-1840, 6½ high petal socket, loop design on base two pieces - wafer joined**
Colors: Canary (shown), crystal, vaseline, opaque white, translucent white (clambroth), mo onstone, translucent powder-blue, opaque light blue, clear turquoise or sky blue, light peacock-blue, light grass green, clear sea green, emerald green, dark bluish green, light bluish gray, translucent soft yellow green, translucent white base - translucent blue socket. Current value, $75.00 - 100.00.

**The "Merese", commonly known as "Wafer" or "Button", was applied while still fluid or plastic enough to attach firmly to the parts of the item to be joined. It was used to join stem to base, socket to stem, as well as in connection parts of stem to shaft.

1   2   3   4   5

6   7   8   9

10   11   12   13   14

8. Petticoat Dolphin, circa 1860-1870, 6¼″ high.
   This Dolphin has been listed in various publication made by three glass manufacturers: Boston and Sandwich, Bakewell, Pears & Co., and McKee Brothers. We are going to exclude the first two and stay with McKee Brothers again. As with Item 6 above, it is important to untangle the problem in researching the Petticoat Dolphin. McKearin's *American Glass* lists it as made by McKee Brothers and we are convinced that McKee is the manufacturer. In 1925-1935, Heisey issued a Petticoat Sandwich Dolphin. It was a close copy of the one shown. Heisey colors were crystal, flamingo, and green. Colors: Light peacock-blue with opalescent rims, light canary with opalescent rims. Current value, $300.00 - 350.00.

9. Mushroom Base, 1930-1940, 7″ high.
   This candlestick presented research problems for it has a "New England" type socket, yet Sandwich made one like it with a mushroom base, which is typical Sandwich. Both are joined with a wafer. (See item 7 above for wafer definition). No listing has been found, but Caleton Brown (of the Ford Museum, Dearborn, Mich.) felt sure that it was Sandwich. Mckearin (392-57) lists it but has no reference to its origin. Colors: crystal (shown), clear sea green. Current value, $100.00 - 125.00.

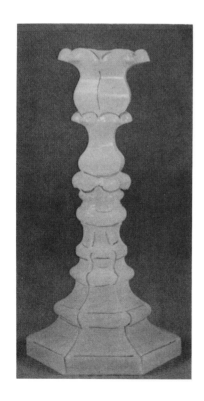

10&12. Petal-Top Column, circa 1840-1850, 9¼″ High.
   Also referred to as Doric Column. Colors: crystal and clambroth (shown), brilliant yellow green, canary yellow, translucent powdery violet, opaque frosted blue, opaque white (not clambroth), opaque white base - translucent blue socket, translucent-frosted pale orchid, opaque white base - pale apple green socket. Can also be found with gold decorations on base. Current Value, $100.00 - 135.00.

11. Petal-Top, Mushroom Base, circa 1835-1840, 7⅜″ high wafer joined.
   Colors: Clambroth (shown), crystal, canary yellow, periwinkle blue, light peacock blue, deep amethyst, light emerald green. Current value, $175.00 - 225.00.

13&14. Petal-Top, Christmas Tree Base, circa 1840-1850, 7″ high, wafer joined.
   Colors: clambroth and crystal (shown), canary, frosted opaque white, clambroth base - translucent blue top, opaque white base - translucent blue top, opaque white base - translucent apple green top, opaque white rose - opaque blue top. Current value, $175.00 - 230.00.

BOSTON & SANDWICH

New England

1,3,5. Crucifix, circa 1850-1865, 11½″ high.
Narrow relief band at the top of cross bearing the letters "INRI". Larger Sandwich Crucifix candlesticks may have the letters "IHS" that sometimes appear in gilt. Other publications have shown this candlestick as a New England Glass Company product, but we made two trips to the Sandwich Glass Museum, Sandwich, Mass., to study Sandwhich Glass and we are sure of the identification of this article. The Sandwich Historical Society lists this item on page 21, Item 1 of the *Glass Exhibit in the Sandwich Glass Museum,* Nimrod Press, Boston, 1969. Colors: Opaque white and pink (shown). The pink is very rare. Other known colors are intense blue green, emerald green, translucent medium blue, citron, translucent powder blue. Possibly may be found in jade green. Current value, $300.00 - 375.00.

2&4. Special Order, circa 1830-1835, 10″ high without shade.
Shades are not original. Octagonal pestle stem on a square plinth with beveled edges and chamfered corners. Shade ring is pot-metal, very rough socket. Believed to be a special order, possibly one of a kind. We know the base is the typical sandwich base used for whale-oil lamps. The stem is wafer joined to a free-blown ring-holder and socket. The original shades were most likely straight cylinder hurricane shades, possibly flared at the top. Current value, $200.00 - 225.00.

6. Double Knop Stem, Step Base, circa 1830-1840, 8¼″ high.
Pressed step base with free blown double knop stem and socket. Socket has pewter candle cup for easy removal of candle stub, helping save the melted wax which was reused. Also known as Lacy step base. We know of no other colors. Current value, $100.00 - 125.00.

7. Crucifix, circa 1830, 9″ high.
We have attributed this item to Sandwich because of its make-up and rare color (believed to be experimental). There are so many Crucifixes, and in the case of sandwich, many sizes and shapes were made. Nevertheless, this candlestick is typical New England Glass, therefore we must leave room to classify it as either Sandwich or New England Glass Co. Current value, $185.00 - 230.00

8. Peacock Eyes, circa 1830-1840, 8″ high.
Name derived from pattern on base. Pressed base with free blown double knop socket. No other colors known. Current value, $100.00 - 130.00

9. Hexagonal Socket - Plinth Base, Circa 1830-1840, 7½″ high, wafer joined.
Unlike the free blown stem and socket of Items 1&3, we have a pressed top and bottom, joined with a wafer. The base is the same as items 1&3. This hexagonal socket has bothered us, as New England Glass Company often used the same design. The key is that New England did not make a wafer joined candlestick (that we are aware of); Sandwich, Bakewell, and Bakewell & Pears did. This fact has helped us unravel some of the so-called New England area glass. Colors: flint crystal (shown), canary. Current value, $175.00 - 200.00

10. Uno-Hexagon, circa 1850-1888, 7″ high. Can also be found 9″ high.
We have named this "Uno" (number one) because it seems to have been the number one candlestick of the New England Glass Company. It is easier to obtain than any of the best. Maybe "easy" is not a good word — it's hard to find any New England area glass today. Colors: clambroth (translucent white) shown. Other known colors are canary, crystal, vaseline, grass green, medium blue, sapphire-blue (sometimes called lavender blue), greenish blue, rose-amethyst, deep amethyst. Current value, $100.00 - 130.00

New England
New England Glass Company
1818-1888

11. Round Base, circa 1850-1860, 7½" high.
We have some reservations about this stick as it has properties that are contradictions to previous statements regarding the New England Glass Co. First, it is a wafer-joined candlestick, yet the basic shape is New England Glass Company. Second, it is also typical of Sandwich glass, but the texture of the glass is wrong. Therefore, we must classify it as being just "New England Area." Now, in order to not leave you hanging, all roads point to it being from Jarves and Cormerais of South Boston (the firm later became Mt. Washington Glass Co. of New Bedford, Mass). No other colors are known. Current value, $85.00 - 95.00

12. Hexagon-Solid, circa 1870-1880, 9" high.
Identification of this candlestick has been difficult. At this time, we can only attribute it to the New England Glass Company. This is based on the shape, glass texture, and the fact that it is a one-piece molded candlestick. We believe that it was a very early product of the period indicated, 1870-1880. No information on other colors has been discovered. Current value, $80.00 - 100.00

13&14. Crucifix, No. 1336, circa 1868, 10" high.
Untangling the Crucifix candlesticks has been a difficult task. Some of the bases are identical, while the sockets, crosses and figures are totally different. We have a number of Crucifix candlesticks we believe were made by the New England Glass Company, but this is the only one which appears in a catalog of theirs, dated 1868. Colors: translucent blue and opaque white. We have had a translucent green with gold decoration. Current value, $150.00 - 235.00

BOSTON & SANDWICH
New England

1

2

3

4

5

6

7

8

9

10

11

12

13

14

*3500/32.   6½ in. Candelabrum
With Bobeche and Prisms*

3500/31.   6 in. Candlestick

1 & 3. No. 1273, circa 1920-1930, 9½" high. Can also be found 7" high as No. 1271.
Colors: jade and ivory hand-enameled (shown), primrose, heliotrope, and azurite. Current value item 1, $50.00 - 60.00; Current value item 3, $75.00 - 100.00

2. No. 64, Cambridge Arms, circa 1930-1953.
Consisting of: No. 628 Low Candlestick (1), No. 1563-4 Candle Arms (1), No. 1536 Peg Nappie (3), additional arms shown on plate #5. Current value $80.00 - 110.00

4. No. 66, Nearcut Special Article, circa 1920-1930, 6" high. Can be found 7" high and will be No. 67.
Other listings for the same pattern: No. 200/22 Nearcut 6" high, No. 200/23 Nearcut 6" high, No. 200/24 Nearcut 7" high, No. 200/25 Nearcut 7" high. The difference between these listings is unknown to us. We do know that No. 200/22 & 24 was made for cutting, copper wheel engraving and deep plate etching. Known deep plate etchings are: P.E. 530, Known cuttings are: No. 2195 and No. 4077. Colors: crystal (shown), azurite, and ebony. Current value, $22.00 - 26.00

5. No. 3500/32, Candelabrum, circa 1933-1940, 6½" high.
Known as 3500. "Gadroon" Line was made without bobeche and prisms as No. 3500/31, 6½" high; can also be found 4" high as No. 3500/74. A rare version of this candlestick can be found with the "Gadroon Rams Head" on two sides of the socket. Colors: crystal with gold encrustation (deposit) shown. Other known colors are Crown Tuscan, amber, peachglo, amethyst, carman, dianthus pink, emerald-dark, forest green, mandarin gold, moonlight blue, royal blue, ebony, and milk. Current value, $40.00 - 50.00

6. Cambridge glass advertising sign known as a "Shelf Sign". (Color added for photographing). No value placed.

7. No. 3121, Candelabra, circa 1949-1953, 7½" high.
No other listings known. Colors: crystal with gold encrustation shown. We do not know of any other colors. Occasionally found with etching on bases and bobeches. Current value, $35.00 - 40.00

Caprice 1338
3 lite Candlestick

8&9. Classic, 7″ and 8½″ high.
Although these candlesticks were displayed in a museum as Cambridge, and we are still listing them as such, we have not been able to obtain documentation as to their true identity. Current value, $18.00 - 26.00

10. No. 1338, 3-Light, circa 1933-1950, 6″ high.
Also listed as: No. 3400-1338 3 holder Candelabrum, No. 3500-1338 "Gadroon" Line Candelabrum. Used for the following patterns: Roslyn-1338 3-Light, Caprice-1338 3-Light, (etchings on underside of base). Colors: crystal (shown), amber, dianthus, moonlight, emerald, royal blue, carman, mandarin gold, milk glass. Current value, $25.00 - 35.00

11. No. 646, Ring Stem - Decagon Base.
For details, see Plate 9. We did not have this item when Plate 9 was photographed and felt that it was important to show it because of the color, heatherbloom (very difficult color to find in this pattern). Current value, $45.00 - 55.00

12. No. 3, "Everglade" 2-holder, circa 1933-1945.
Later date re-numbered as No. 1211, also known as "Leafline" No. 1216. Can be found in a single-holder as No. 1209. Colors: crystal (shown), carman, moonlite blue, and emerald green. Current value, $25.00 - 35.00

13. No. 2777 Mission "Nearcut", circa 1903-1920, 7″ high.
No other listings known. Colors: crystal shown. No other colors known. Current value, $18.00 - 22.00

1338. Candelabrum

1211 Candelabra

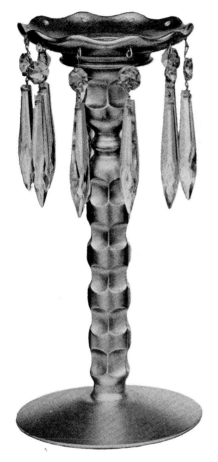

1269-11"

1273-10½"

1271-7"

1270-6½"

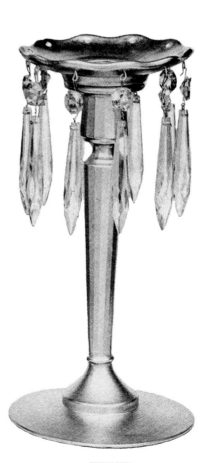

1272-10½"

Crown Tuscan

1,2,3.   Console Set, circa 1949-1953.
      Consists of: No. 50 Dolphin (2) 8″ high, No. SS40 flower or fruit center (1). Current value items 1 and 3, $75.00 - 90.00, current value item 2, $120.00 - 130.00

4&8.   No. 66, Footed Dolphin, 4″ high.
      Also listed as No. SS66 "Coral". Current value, $60.00 - 70.00

5,6,7.   Console Set.
      Consists of: 2-light dolphin (2), 5″ high. No. SS21 footed candy box & cover (1). Current value items 5 and 7, $40.00 - 45.00, current value item 6, $50.00 - 60.00

9,10,11.   Rose Point Console Set.
      22 karat gold encrustation, consists of: No. 647 2-light (2), 6″ high, No. 3400/48 bowl (1). Current value items 9 and 11, $50.00 - 55.00, current value item 10, $65.00 - 85.00

Cambridge Arms

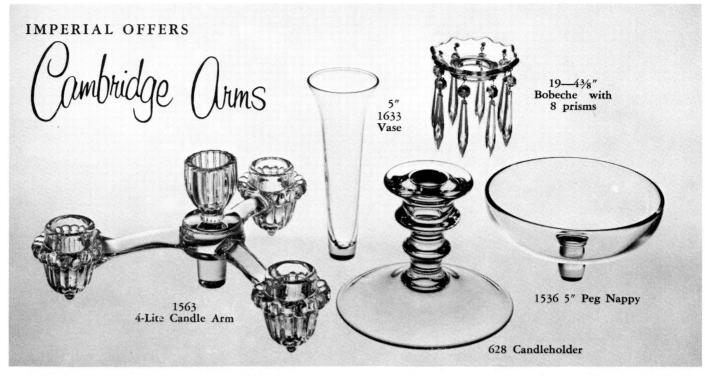

5"
1633
Vase

19—4⅜"
Bobeche with
8 prisms

1563
4-Lite Candle Arm

628 Candleholder

1536 5" Peg Nappy

#42/6

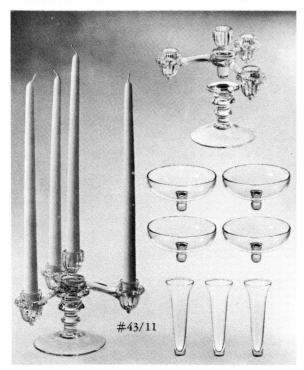

#43/11

Cambridge Arms

The Most Versatile Centerpiece Ever Conceived
America loves and wants Cambridge Arms—graceful, crystal decorative table accessories so adaptable to the creation of unique, clever arrangements. Cambridge Arms permits SO MANY unusual groupings—from simple centerpiece to a most elaborate table decoration.

SWEETMEAT TREE 6 Piece Set

For Cocktail Nuts & Tid-Bits, Sweetmeats & All Candies, Caviar & Seafood Spreads, Cheesé Dips, Buffet Relishes & Condiments, Sweets & Sours, Jellies, Jams & Preserves at Buffet and Hunt Breakfasts, Gourmet Pickle Server, "USAGE HORIZONS" unlimited! Suggest a Candle in Center Hole or flowers in the Vase when being used as described and feature for use as a four-Candle Holder for the Dining Table.

VERSATILITY SET 11 Piece Unit

This is the Senior Set in famed Cambridge Arms —a sparkling new idea in table center decorative arrangements! SCORES of DIFFERENT centerpieces can be put together with these gleaming crystal-clear glass items. Consumers can do countless plain, simple, casual or elaborate arrangements with the parts in this Set—"VARIETY IS THE SPICE" in Table Settings!

**Cambridge Arms Ad
Crockery & Glass Journal
May 1961**

1. No. 1612/1614, Dolphin Hurricane Lamp, circa 1920-1930, 16″ high. Also found 18″ high as No. 1612/1615 colors: crystal shown. Other known colors are Crown Tuscan, milk glass. Current value, $125.00 - 135.00

2. Cambridge Arms, Royal Blue Base, Arms shown consists of the following:
   No. 628 low candlestick (1), No. 1563-4 candle arms (2), No. 1633 peg vase (3). Interesting to note that in the National Cambridge Collectors, Inc. book - years 1949 thru 1953, 36 different arrangements of cambridge arms are shown. Current value, $90.00 - 120.00

3&4. Clear Pattern, circa 1920-1930, 7″ and 12″ high.
   No catalog listing has been found for these candlesticks. They were identified as Cambridge in Bennett's *The Cambridge Glass Book*. They are only shown in crystal and we have no other listing. Current value item 3, $18.00 - 24.00, current value item 4, $30.00 - 35.00

5. No. P-499, Calla Lilly, circa 1949-1953, 6½″ high.
   No other listing known. Used for the following patterns: Thistle-rock crystal cutting No. 1066. Silver Maple - rock crystal cutting No. 1067. Colors: forest green (shown), amber, apple green, crystal, emerald, heatherbloom, moonlight, and ebony. Current value, $25.00 - 30.00

6. No. 1595, circa 1920-1930, 9″ high.
   Can be found with No. 19 bobeche and 8 No. 1 3″ high prisms. Listed as 1595 Candelabra. Colors: mulberry (shown), amber, apple green, crystal. Current value, $34.00 - 38.00

7. No. 70 With Prisms, circa 1949-1953, 7″ high.
   Also known as C-70 Candelabra. Colors: moonlight with satin finish on base shown. Other known colors are crystal and amber. Current value, $25.00 - 30.00

8. No. 1192, circa 1930-1940, 6″ high.
   Other known listings are: No. 34/1192 - 3400 Line Plate Etched (No. 746 "Gloria"), No. 1270 Lustre Cut Prism candlestick with patented lock bobeche 6½″ high. Colors: amethyst with silver over-lay (shown), crystal, moonlight blue, crown tuscan, carmen, and peachglo. Current value, $18.00 $26.00

3400/1192-6″ Candle

9. No. 1307, 3-Lite Candelabra, circa 1930-1950, 5″ high.
Only one other known listing which is called a candelabrum instead of a candelabra (do not confuse this item with No. 1545 3-light candlestick. The base and height are different). This item was used with console sets and can be found with etched and decorated patterns on the base. Examples are as follows: etching no. E/764 with No. 1349 bowl, decoration No. D/997 with no. 993 bowl, decoration No. D/999 with No. 993 bowl. Colors: azure blue (azurite) shown. The other known color is Crown Tuscan. Current value $30.00 - 35.00

10,11,12. Cambridge Nude - No. 3011, circa 1935-1953, 9″ high.
Also known as "Figure" candlestick Colors: Crown Tuscan, crystal, and crystal with forest green socket (shown). Item 11 appears to be tinted; it is, but was accomplished by the sun.* Item 12 is very rare in crystal with an applied color socket. Other known colors are blue mild glass, heliotrope, crystal - satin finish, royal blue, crystal with carman socket. Current value item 10 and 12, $70.00 - 90.00, current value item 11, $55.00 - 65.00.

*Sun colored glass, commonly called desert glass, is also known as purpled glass, turned glass and amethystine glass. This is glass that is clear (crystal) and has colored or turned purplish by exposure to sunlight. Generally speaking, all clear glass produced before 1920, with the exception of flint or lead crystal, will turn amethyst or purplish when exposed to sunlight. The degree or discoloration will depend on the amount of manganese used as a decoloring agent during the making of the glass; also it is totally dependent on length of time for maximum shade, and could take from 2 to 10 years. Such exposure can ruin a pair of candlesticks when one is exposed to sunlight and the other is not.

1307. Candelabrum
E/764

1596
6½ in. Candlestick

1&3.   Petticoat Dolphin, circa 1925-1930, 9½″ high.
Colors: rubina and emerald green (shown), amber, mandarin gold, forest green. A 1926 advertisement listed it available in amber-glo. The rubina petticoat dolphin should be considered one of the rare Cambridge collectible items. I have yet to see one for sale at an antique show or any advertisement of one for sale in any trade papers. This one was found in Boston in a little basement antique shop across from the State House. It had been sitting in the window for over 3 years, never dusted. The dust was so thick that I could not tell that it was not plain crystal. However, I thought that it might be a good one, and brought it home. Believe me, it was almost "Heart-Attack" time when we washed it and found "Rubina" under all the dust & dirt. My point is that there are still important finds in unexpected places, you just have to keep on looking. Current value item 1, $175.00 - 200.00 current value item 3, $85.00 - 100.00

2.   No. 645 3-light, circa 1945-1953, 5″ high.
Do not confuse this item with No. 663 3-light which is used for an epergne base. The No. 645 has licking bobeche for the center socket. The No. 663 has a plain center socket to allow a Cambridge "Arms" to fit flush with the socket. To add to the confusion, there is a No. 1545 3-light, 5½″ high, which has the same sockets but with a bell shaped base. Then we have No. 1307 candelabrum which has the same sockets, but on a taller stem (body). Colors: we are not aware of any colors other than crystal. Current value, $40.00 - 48.00

4,5,6,7.   Column, circa 1930-1940.
We have shown a number of these candlesticks to display the various finishes and colors. Item 4: Green painted and fired shown, but we have seen orange and sky blue. 7″ high. Items 5&6: Rubina and moonlight. 8½″ high. Item 7: amber 9¼″ high. Other known colors are ivory, azurite, jade, ebony, and royal blue. Current value items 4, 5, and 6, $15.00 - 22.00, current value item 7, $22.00 - 26.00.

8,9,10,11,12.   Twists, circa 1931-1940, 8½″ high.
Un-scrambling time! When this plate was photographed, it was our intention to show the difference between the Tiffin (U.S. Glass) twists and the Cambridge twists. We believe now that we have unravelled, or if you will, un-twisted the Cambridge/Tiffin candlesticks. Deduction as follows: Item 8 has no ribbon in the center of the twist as the other candlesticks shown; therefore we had attributed it to Tiffin. Items 9 & 10, we thought were Cambridge (ribbon in middle of twist) but we had trouble with the colors. Item 11, but to the color, apple green with ribbon in the middle of the twist, we felt sure was Cambridge. Item 12, black satin, has the ribbon, but the Cambridge ebony candlesticks have a different finish. Meantime, Fred Bickenhouser released his Tiffin 11 book and the theory that the "Ribbon in the middle of the twist" was made only by Cambridge went out of the window; Tiffin made the same pattern. In July, 1981 at Barbara Shaeffer's "Glass Bash" in Strongsville, Ohio, Phillis and Bill Smith (Cambridge Collectors) and I reached the conclusion that only item 11 was a Cambridge candlestick. This is based on two major findings: (1.) The Tiffin candlesticks are all three-mold and the Cambridge, two-mold candlesticks. (2.) Color can be identified by positively known colors. We had photographed this plate long before we reached the above conclusions, but it gives a better perspective of the various candlesticks, so we felt that it was better to leave it as shown. Solving the twist mystery was well worth the extra effort. (See Plate 49, Items 1,2,4,5, for U.S. Glass - Tiffin twists). Current value items 8,9, and 10, $26.00 - 32.00, current value items 11 and 12, $24.00 - 28.00

1715
Ash Tray

506
4 in. Candelabrum

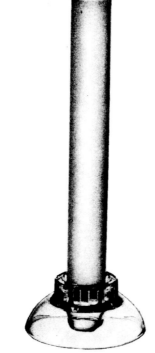

1715
Candleholder

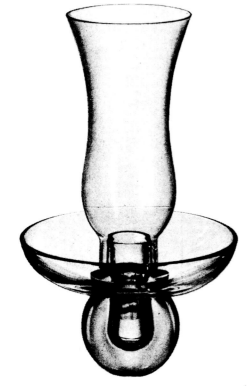

55
Hurricane Lamp

510/1537
Ball Candlestick
& Peg Nappy w/Candlewell

54
Hurricane Lamp

start with these basic
"Cambridge Arms" units

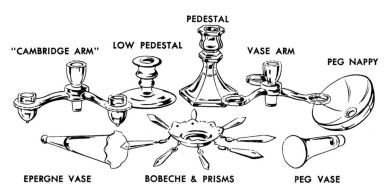

"CAMBRIDGE ARM"   LOW PEDESTAL   PEDESTAL   VASE ARM   PEG NAPPY

EPERGNE VASE   BOBECHE & PRISMS   PEG VASE

Now, for the first time, you can do "tricks" with your table or buffet centerpiece . . . come up with an entirely new and clever arrangement, for every meal! It's all done with unique "Cambridge Arms," the sparkling, interchangeable crystal units shown above. Scores of different decorative settings, from simplest flower holders to elaborate multi-branch candlestick arrangements! Buy in sets or open stock . . . at leading stores. All items in a very moderate price range.

Illustrations at right show single Cambridge Arm as candleholder with flowers; a flower centerpiece (center) is made with one arm, one vase and three dishes; a lovely decorative theme is made with fruit and leaves in a shallow bowl with towering candles rising from a single Cambridge Arm.

It's simple table arithmetic—add or subtract and come up with
a different centerpiece for every meal!

Let these unique
sparkling switchabouts
bring new charm to your table!

You'll get a real thrill out of creating new decorative effects with "Cambridge Arms." The possibilities for novel arrangements are limited only by your own ingenuity!

101 ways
to give your table a
"new look"

Cambridge Arms brochure.

27

1. No. 200/34 Crucifix, circa 1910-1915, 9″ high.
   The candlestick shown was made in a very worn mold. The figure of Christ is distinguishable, but that's about all. The "INRI" which should appear on a small ribbon above the figure (believed to be on all Cambridge Crucifix candlesticks) is not legible at all. Due to the basic shape, we are attributing the one shown to Cambridge. Colors: crystal (shown), milk glass. Current value, $18.00 - 22.00

2. 4 - Candle Centerpiece, circa 1930-1935.
   Shown with No. 509 figure (two kids; kid & kid goat) flower holder. No other listings known. Colors: light emerald green (shown), amber, and dianthus pink. Current value, $125.00 - 150.00

3. No. 1 Crucifix, circa 1903-1910.
   Also known as "Opal Novelties" (1903 catalog). Identified as a "Nearcut" item later date, approximately 1910. Colors: milk glass (shown), believed to have been manufactured in crystal also. Current value, $24.00 - 30.00

4. No. 2630, Colonial "Nearcut", circa 1903-1910, 7″ high.
   Can also be found 9″ high. Do not confuse this with No. 2657. The sockets are different, the bases are the same. No other listings known. Colors: crystal shown, no other colors known. Current value, $20.00 - 24.00

5. Paden City No. 114.
   Shown for comparison. The most easily discerned difference is in the top of the socket. The Paden City socket is thicker than the Cambridge. Current value, $18.00 - 22.00

6. No. 200/16, "Nearcut", circa 1903-1930, 6″ high.
   Details listed with Items 9, 10, & 11 below. Current value, $18.00 - 22.00

7. No. 73, Special Article "Nearcut", circa 1903-1930, 6½″ high.
   Made for cutting. Other listings: No. 200/26 "Nearcut" 6½″ high* No. 200/27 "Nearcut" 6½″ high; No. 200/26-27 was also made for cut, copper wheel engraving and deep plate etching. Cuttings known: No. 4099 and 896, Copper wheel engraving: No. 5011, Deep plate etching: No. 529 No. 916 "Nearcut" 6½″ high. (This was a very early listing, believed to be around 1903). Colors: crystal (shown), azurite and ebony. See Plate 39, Items 11 & 12, New Martinsville No. 12 (look-a-like).

8. No. 66, "Nearcut" Special Article.
   Details are listed for this item on Plate 3, Item 4. Current value, $22.00 - 26.00.

9,10,11. No. 200/18, "Nearcut", circa 1903-1930, 7″ high.
   Can also be found as follows: No. 200/17 - 6″ high, No. 200/19 - 7″ high. Another catalog listed the same candlesticks as follows: No. 200/16 - 6½″ high, No. 200/18 - 7½″ high. These last listings were candlesticks made for deep plate etching. No. P.E. 510. No. 200/16 - 18 was made for cut and copper wheel engraving. Examples of copper wheel engraving are No. 5017 and No. 5018. Also No. 2862 "Nearcut", 6¼″ high. We have not untangled the difference, if any, between No. 200/16 - 18 and No. 200/17 - 19. Colors: Item 6 - crystal with silver deposit, Item 9 - crystal with encrustation decoration (decoration believed to be by Lotus). Item 10 - crystal with cutting (cutting unknown), other known colors are amber, apple green, azurite, azure blue, emerald, heliotrope, jade and primrose. Item 11 - Duncan No. 66 shown for comparison. Notice ballast in stem is shaped different. Under-base is deeper than Cambridge candlestick. For detail see Plate 11, Item 4. Current value, $18.00 - 22.00

12. No. 200/6 7½″ high (see Plate 10, Item 1). Current value, $18.00 - 22.00.

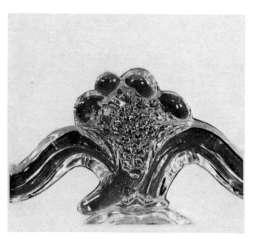

No. 658/2 Center Horn-of-Plenty

No. 3500/95 Center Rams Head

1,2,&3. No. 65 Doric Column, circa 1920-1930, 9½″ high.
"Nearcut" Special Articles Console Set with 3500 "Gadroon" line Rams Head Bowl*. Colors: ebony shown with 22 karat gold encrustation (coin gold encrustation listed in 1922 advertisement). Other known colors are azurite, jade, crystal, amber, milk glass, royal blue, forest green, amethyst, dianthus pink and ivory. The 1922 advertisement listed the sticks shown as "Ebony Art Ware". Current value Items 1 and 3, $35.00 - 45.00 current value Item 2, $95.00 - 115.00.

*Although we do not intend to research the bowls shown with console sets, this one should be of special interest to Cambridge Collectors. A close look will reveal that the bowl rim is round and smooth and does not have a ruffled edge as the 3500 "Gadroon" Line 3500/25 bowl.

4. No. 68, Special Article "Newcut", circa 1920-1930, 10″ high.
Made for cutting. Other listing: No 200/1 "Nearcut" - For cut and copper wheel engraving. Can be found with cutting No. 4077 and copper wheel engraving No. 5013. Can be found 7½″ high and will be No. 200/2 "Nearcut". Both 200/1 and 200/2 were used for deep plate etching pattern No. 510. Colors: ebony shown with coin gold encrustation. Other known colors are azurite, crystal, primrose, and heliotrope. Current value, $30.00 - 35.00

5. No. 658/2, 2-Light Candelabra, circa 1920-1935, 6″ high.
Shown with No. 19 bobeches and 16 No. 1 prisms. Can be found with No. 27 bobeche (round edges) and 12 No. 5 prisms. This is listed as No. 658/1 candelabrum. Colors: cyrstal (shown). We are not aware of any other colors. Current value, $35.00 - 45.00

6. No. 3500/95, 2 Holder Candelabra, circa 1930-1935, 6½″ high.
Shown with No. 19 bobeches and 16 No. 1 prisms. If found without bobeches (no holding ring on sockets) it will be No. 3500/94. This candlestick is commonly referred to as the "Rams Head" stick. Colors: crystal shown. We are not aware of any other colors. Current value, $35.00 - 45.00

3500/95. 2 Holder
with Bobèches and Prisms

3500/94. 2 Holder

7. No. 70, "Nearcut", circa 1920-1930, 8″ high.
   Special article made for cutting in azurite, ebony and crystal. Made for cutting: No. 200/5 "Nearcut" made for cutting, copper wheel engraving and deep plate etching. Typical patterns can be found in copper wheel engraving No. 5012 and deep plate etching No. 530. No. 102 dresden "Nearcut", deep plate etched. Colors: ebony shown with coin gold encrustation. Other known colors are azurite, crystal and primrose current value, $30.00 - 35.00

8. No. 1358, 3 Holder Candelabra, circa 1934-1953, 7″ high.
   With bobeches and prisms. The bobeches have "Lock" notches and raised holder on sockets. Can be found with 2-vase ringed "arm" and will be known as No. 1358 3-Light Epergne (see item 10 for arm & vase). No other listing known. Colors: crystal shown. We know of no other colors. Current value, $40.00 - 45.00

9. No. 2750 2-Handle "Nearcut", circa 1910-1920, 7″ high.
   No other listings known. Colors: crystal shown. No other colors known. Current value, $20.00 - 26.00

10. No. 1357, 3 Lite Epergne, circa 1934-1953, 7″ high.
    In a 1934 catalog, No. 1357 was listed as 3 holder. The 3 light epergne appears in a 1949-1953 catalog. This applies to item 8 (No. 1358). No other listings known. Colors: crystal shown. We know of no other colors. Current value, $60.00 - 70.00

Ring Stem

Victorian Candelabra
6678—With all the eclat of the last century, se clear crystal candelabra can dignify any-'s mantel or table. Two branched, with crys-pendants. 12¾ in. high $15.00 pair

Plate No. 9 is dedicated to one basic candlestick design. As can be seen, the design ranges from a single socket, to 2-light and 3-light candelabras. The National Cambridge Collectors, Inc. members refer to the design as "Ring Stem", therefore we feel that it should be known as such. The use of the Ring Stem design for patterns and cuttings must be the most used of any candlestick by Cambridge. Due to this, we are changing the reference format to simplify and identify the use of the design. First, we have listed the candlestick shown; second, we have taken each candlestick by catalog number and pattern to keep from repeating so much information on each candlestick. The Ring Stem candlesticks were produced from 1930 to 1953. Total colors were as follows: royal blue, carmen, heatherbloom, amber, moonlight blue, Crown Tuscan and ebony.

Candlesticks shown:

1&3. No. 647, Crown Tuscan, 6″ high. Current value, $50.00 - 55.00

2. No. 38, Mt. Vernon Candelabrum, 13½″ high, crystal. Current value, $60.00 - 75.00

4&7. No. 646, 6″ high, crystal and ebony. Current value, $30.00 - 35.00

5&6. No. 638, Candelabra, 6½″ high, ebony and crystal. Current value, $35.00 - 45.00

8,9,10. No. 647, Console Set, 6″ high, gold encrested (22 karat gold). Current value items 8 and 10, $45.00 - 50.00. Current value item 9, $85.00 - 95.00

See Plate 3, item 11, for a No. 647 heatherbloom.

Patterns using the Ring Stem design

Caprice: No. 646 and No. 647
Crown Tuscan: No. 646 and No. 647
Rose Point: No. 646 and No. 647
Candlelight: No. 1603 Hurricane lamp (No. 646 with bobeche, prisms, and Hurricane shade) No. 647 (losted as no. 3400/647) any Candlelight candlestick should be considered very rare.
Portia: No. 1603 Hurricane lamp
Roselyn: No. 646 and No. 647
Bexley No. 647 - Rock Crystal cutting No. 1053
Harvest No. 647 - Rock Crystal cutting No. 1053
King Edward No. 647 - Rock Crystal cutting No. 821
Belfast No. 647 - Rock Crystal cutting No. 942
Celestial No. 647 - Rock Crystal cutting No. 600 (listed as No. 600/647)
Windsor No. 647 - Rock Crystal cutting No. 500 (listed as No. 500/647)
Ivy No. 647 - Rock Crystal cutting No. 1059
Granada No. 647 - Rock Crystal cutting No. 1068
Apple Blossom No. 647 (listed as 3400/647) - 3400 Line etching No. 744
No. 646 (listed as 3400/646), No. 638 (listed as 3400/638)
Decagon No. 638 Candelabra - etching No. 739
Spring Time console set No. 646 (used with No. 1256 oval bowl)

Table Centers - Console Sets

The table centers and console sets were a major part of the use of the Ring Stem Pattern. Most were sold with flower figures or flower holders. Rather than list these, we will give you some idea of their use. The National Cambridge Collectors books show most of the sets, and if further information is desired, these books should be consulted. No. 638 used with 5 sets, No. 646 used with 4 sets, No. 647 used with 5 sets. If you compound these sets by using each pattern with the various bowls and figure flower holders, you can get a combination of 196 different sets.

Ring Stem

Gold & Silver Decorated Ware

Silver: No. 638 decoration No. D/971-S, No. 646 decoration No. D/971-S Gold: Decoration pattern No. D/450 was used on the following: No. 646, No. 647, No. 648/19 Candelabra, No. 1268 2-light Candelabra. Most of the gold decorations were on ebony items.

Etched & Engraved Items

Diane - 3400 Dinnerware - plate etched No. 752, No. 646 (listed as 3400/646), No. 647 (listed as 3400/647), No. 638 (listed as 3400/638) Rock crystal engraved - No. 647 Candelabrum - engraved No. 644, No. 1268 Prism Candelabrum - engraved No. 629, No. 1268 Lustre Prism Candelabrum - engraved No. 621, No. 647 Candelabrum - engraved "Laurel Wreath" Mount Vernon: No. 38 candelabrum with No. 1 prisms

1

2

3

4

5

6

7

8

9

10

38
13½" Candelabrum
No. 1 Prism

1274-13½" 2-Light
Lustre Cut Prism Candelabrum

646-5" Candlestick

1268 2-Light
Lustre Cut Prism Candelabrum

1274-13½" 2-Light
Lustre Cut Prism Candelabrum
Rock Crystal Engraved 560

647 Candelabra

638 Candelabra

647

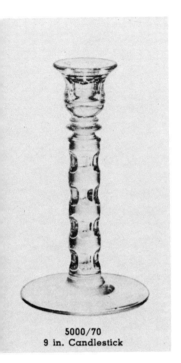

5000/70
9 in. Candlestick

HEIRLOOM

5000/68
4½ in. Candlestick

5000/67
3½ in. Candlestick

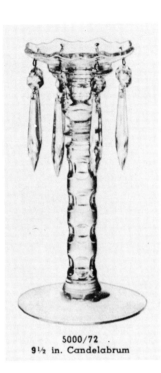

5000/72
9½ in. Candelabrum

67
5 in. Candlestick

72
6 in. 2 lite Candlestick

67
5 in. Candlestick

68
5 in. Candlestick

35
8″ Candlestick

130
4″ Candlestick

36
8½″ Lustre Cut Prism
Candlestick, No. 2 Prism

1. This candlestick has 4 numbers listed, Circa 1920-1930, 7½″ high.
No. 200/7 "Nearcut" Made for cutting and copper wheel engraving and deep plate etching. It can be found in a variety of each such as plate etching No. 510, cutting No. 4048, and cutting No. 4085, also copper wheel engraving No. 5009.
No. 71 "Nearcut" made for cutting in azurite, ebony and crystal.
No. 2800 community crystal No. 235 "Nearcut".
No. 1440 candleabra (with bobeche and prisms). 1940 catalog listings: No. 1440/1 No. 19 bobeche and 8 No. 1 3″ prisms. No. 1440/2 No. 19 bobeche and 8 No. 1 2″ prisms. No. 1440/5 No. 20 bobeche and 10 No. 1 5″ prisms. Colors: primrose (shown), azurite and/or azure blue, ebony, heliotrope, jade and crystal. A crystal No. 200/6 is shown on Plate 7, item 12. Current value, $35.00 - 40.00

2&4. This candlestick has 5 numbers listed, circa 1920-1930, 7″ high.
No. 2750 "Nearcut" Listed as: extra fine colonial quality, full finished.
No. 2859 "Nearcut".
No. 72 "Nearcut" made for cutting in azurite, ebony and crystal.
No. 200/20 & 200/21 "Nearcut" we are not aware that there is any difference between the two candlesticks. Colors: crystal shown with cutting No. 894. Other known colors are azurite, ebony, heliotrope, ivory, jade and primrose. Current value, $25.00 - 30.00

3. No. 76, Caprice Epergne (Arms with 2 bud-vases for center socket removed).
Patent numbers listed as No. 1977816 & No. 105954. Colors: crystal (shown), moonlight blue. Current value, $50.00 - 60.00

5. No. 35, "Mount Vernon", circa 1930-1933, 8″L high.
Other catalog listings:
Mount Vernon No. 36/19 8½″ high No. 19 bobeche and 8 No. 1 3″ prisms.
Mount Vernon No. 36/20/1 No. 20 bobeche and 10 No. 1 3″ prisms.
Mount Vernon No. 36/20/2 No. 20 bobeche and 10 No. 2 prisms. This candlestick can be found without the diamond-points on the column (stick body) and will be listed as No. 200/4 8″ high. Other than a single candlestick, the 200/4 was used for the following: No. 23 "Cambridge Arms": base, No. 653 "Cambridge Arms" base, No. 657 7-light candelabrum base, No. 1613 17″ hurricane lamp base. Colors: Forest green (shown), amber, carmen, crystal, heatherbloom, mandarin gold, pistachio, royal blue, Crown Tuscan, and milk glass. Current value, $60.00 - 65.00

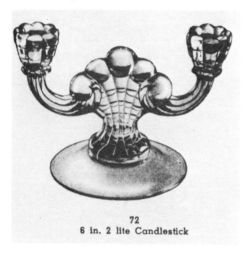

72
6 in. 2 lite Candlestick

6&7. Caprice No. 67, circa 1930's, 2½" high.
Colors: moonlight and amethyst (shown), royal blue, emerald green, amber, dianthus pink, crystal, larosa, mandarin gold, mocha, pistachio, royal blue, Crown Tuscan and milk glass. Current value $12.00 - 16.00

8. No. 2759, 5" Miniature Candelabra, circa 1910-1920.
Known as a 3 prong candlestick when made. Crystal shown. No other color known. Current value, $25.00 - 30.00

9. Cambridge "Shelf" Sign.
The shelf advertisement sign is amber with gold letters (22 karat). These items are very difficult to find, especially the one shown. Should be considered a rare find. No value placed.

10. No. 2798, Birthday Candlestick, circa 1910-1920, 3" high.
Also known as No. 200/9 "Nearcut" crystal shown. No other color known.
This type miniature candlestick was used at each placesetting for a birthday party. Each guest would make a "wish" for the person having the birthday and then blow out the candle. I like it better than having them on the cake. This way one does not give one's age away. Current value, $18.00 - 22.00

11,12,13. Star 2½" high, 4" high, 5" high.
Colors: moonlight (shown), crystal. Current value $12.00 - 18.00

14. 3900 Line Corinth, circa 1949-1953, No. 72, 6" high 2-light Candlestick.
Other listings: No. 2900/72 Rock Crystal "Laurel Wreath" (Molded Laurel Wreath in base)

Deep Plate Etched Patterns in Base
No. 3900/72 "Daffodil", No. 3900/72 "Candlelight", No. 3900/72 "Chantilly", No. 3900/72 "Diane". Others without numbers: Elaine, Portia, Wildflower

Cuttings in Base - Rock Crystal
No. 3900/72 "Achilles" Cut No. 698, No. 3900/72 "Adonis" cut No. 720, No. 3900/72 "Carnation" cut No. 732, No. 3900/72 cut No. 1064 (no name listed), No. 3900/72 cut No. 1065 (no name listed), No. 3900/72 "Thistle" cut No. 1066, No. 3900/72 "Silver Maple" cut No. 1067.
Colors: moonlight-frosted (shown), amber, crystal, emerald, heatherbloom, Crown Tuscan, and ebony. Current value, $30.00 - 35.00

1402/80
6½ in. Candlestick

1402/81
6½ in. Candelabrum
Bobeche and Prisms

15&16. No. 627, 3400 Line, circa 1930-1953, 4″ high.
Other listings: No. 2 "Martha Washington" pattern, No. 2 "Victorian Period" Glassware

Deep Plate Etching On Base
No. 627 "Decagon" No. 731, No. 627 "Decagon Line" No. 738, No. 627 Plate etching No. 739, No. 627 "Cleo" design, No. 627 "Gloria" No. 746

Rock Crystal Engraved
No. 3400/627 pattern No. 541, No. 3400/627 pattern No. 542, No. 627 pattern No. 515, No. 627 pattern No. 530, No. 627 pattern No. 534 assortment, No. 627 pattern No. 644.

This candlestick may also be found with two-tone items such as No. 3400/28 Compote or No. 1236 8″ High Ivy Ball. Listed as "Cambridge" two-tone "quick sellers". Colors: moonlight and ebony (shown), amethyst, carman, crystal, emerald, dianthus pink, forest green and royal blue. Current value, $15.00 - 22.00

17. No. 74, 3900 Line Corinth 3-Light, circa 1930-1953, 6″ high.
Can be found with "Arms" and bud vases. This is No. 75 Epergne.
Other listings:

Deep Plate Etching
No. 3900/74 "Chantilly", No. 3900/74 "Rose Point", No. 3900/74 "Candlelight", No. 3900/74 "Diane", No. 3900/74 "Elaine", No. 3900/74 "Portua", No. 3900/74 "Wildflower", No. 3900/74 "Daffodil". Current value, $25.00 - 30.00

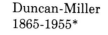

1&3. No. 1 1-Light Candlebrum, circa 1900-1960, 10″ high with "U" prisms. (The 1900 is a guess.)
We think that this pattern might be earlier as this and item 3 carry the same number No. 1. It is not shown in the Bon S-1900 catalog. The lowest numbered candlestick in it is No. 54. Therefore we believe that item 1,2,&3 were made first, before 1900. The reason we say made first, is this candlestick (No. 1&3) was reissued in 1959 by U.S. Glass Co. as No. 41-124. We have another listing for No. 1-41. This we believe was about 1924-1925 when Duncan-Miller first produced the Early American Sandwich Glass Pattern. The No. 1 1-light was added to the sandwich line earlier than 1924. The 1-light was also made as a hurricane lamp using a N. 505 chimney (hurricane shade). The shades were decorated with patterns as Adoration, First Love and Passion Flower. Current value, $35.00 - 40.00

2. No. 1 3-Light Candelabrum, circa 1900-1960, 24″ high 18″ wide with "U" prisms.
We usually are able to list each part of a candelabrum. In the case of the Duncan-Miller candlesticks, we cannot. Most of the parts - ferrules, bobeches, sockets, etc. all fit any given item and can be interchanged easily. There is one additional No. 1 candelabrum 5-light 24″ high, 18″ wide. Colors: crystal (shown). No other color known. Current value, $450.00 - 500.00

4. No. 66, circa 1900-1950, 6″ high.
Also made 4″ & 7½″ high. This shape candlestick was made by a number of glass companies. It is very difficult to pin down the exact manufacturer. We have shown this article in black glass (deep amethyst) because it matches the Francis Bones 1900 catalog better than any we have. We have no knowledge of the colors that Duncan-Miller made in this pattern. We must state that the black glass leads us to a toss-up with Paden City, but the size is wrong for Paden City.

5&6. No. 28, circa 1925-1932, Item 5, 6″ high.
Silver deposit on socket and base. Believed to be decorated by Lotus: Lotus No. 203-DEC 889, Furiste, Modern Trend Design, Patent No. 75, 974. Item 6, 4″ high. Silver deposit on socket and base. Also believed to be decorated by Lotus: Lotus No. 202 Grape Design. We are not aware of any other colors for these two items. Current value, $28.00 - 33.00

7. Daisy and Button Hat, circa 1884, 2½″ high (candle holder in the bottom of the hat).
This is the only article of this type that we have ever seen. We have attributed it to Duncan-Miller, based on the early daisy and button (known in 1884 as Hobnail) items they made. The glass appears to be of this vintage and we are not aware of any other company making daisy and button at this time. Current value, $20.00 - 22.00

8,9,10. No. 41, Low Early American Sandwich, circa 1925-1970's, 4″ high.
The molds for the early American Sandwich pattern were obtained by Indiana Glass Company in 1955 when Duncan-Miller became Duncan-Miller division, U.S. Glass Company. We have no records or have seen no colors in the No. 41 Low Candlestick.
Indiana Glass Co. produced a tall (8½″ high) No. 41 Early American Sandwich Candlestick in amber. Current value, items 8 and 10, $10.00 - 12.00. Current value item 9, $15.00 - 18.00

*Became part of the United States Glass Company in 1955.

1

2

3

4

5

6

7

8

9

10

White Milk Glass

HOBNAIL PATTERN

No. 718-25
4 ½" Candlestick

No. 718-27
Crimped Bowl
Dia: 11 ½"

No. 718-25
4 ½" Candlestick

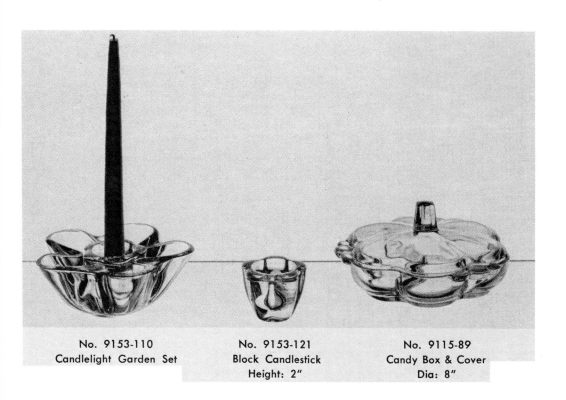

Dawn
by DUNCAN

No. 9153-110
Candlelight Garden Set

No. 9153-121
Block Candlestick
Height: 2"

No. 9115-89
Candy Box & Cover
Dia: 8"

Duncan's Canterbury

PATTERN NUMBER 115

Canterbury is basic stock . . . it gives you practically universal appeal in one line of fine crystal.

Its clean-lined simplicity fits well with contemporary modern. Its classic proportions are good traditional.

Canterbury ware is all hand made, flame polished and hand finished.

The varying thickness of the crystal gives Canterbury unusual light refraction and brilliance. The clarity of the ware, and flawless finish are characteristic of well practised hand craft by the old traditional methods. So, it is satisfying to the eye and to the hand.

HAND-MADE
Duncan

Catalog 93

DUNCAN AND MILLER DIVISION
UNITED STATES GLASS CO., TIFFIN, OHIO

1,2,3. No. 65, Console Set, circa 1900-1950, 11½″ high candlestick.
The flower vase in the epergne is the base of a No. 65 candlestick turned upside down. Either are interchangeable (both fit the same ferrule). In 1910, No. 65 candlestick was issued with a tulip milk glass shade and called a One-Light Candelabra. Again in 1950, revived as pattern No. 120-124. Colors: crystal shown. We have seen one in milk glass. Current value, $40.00 - 50.00

4&5. No. 61, circa 1900, 10″ high.
Made only in crystal as far as we know. Current value, $25.00 - 30.00

6&8. No. 115, Low Magnolia Etching, circa 1940-1950, 3″ high.
Colors: crystal shown. Other colors unknown to us. Other cameo etchings used on this item are "Language of Flowers" and "Indian Tree". Current value, $12.00 - 14.00

7. 2-Light Candelabra, circa 1950, 13″ high.
Can possibly be found in milk glass. In 1950 Duncan-Miller issued a 3-light candelabra in milk glass. It is the same base, same 2-light arm. The only difference is the center spike is removed and a column-candleholder (bobeche and socket) is used in its place. All items connect with standard ferrules. Current value, $50.00 - 60.00

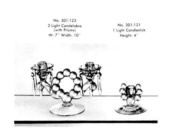

No. 301-123
2 Light Candelabra
(with Prisms)
Ht: 7″ Width: 10″

No. 301-121
1 Light Candlestick
Height: 4″

No. 301-122
2 Light Candlestick
Ht: 6″ Width: 9″

No. 115-123
2 Light Candelabra
Height: 7″

No. 320-124
1 Light Candelabra
Height: 9¼″ Width: 4¼″

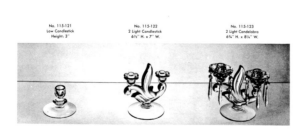

No. 115-121
Low Candlestick
Height: 3″

No. 115-122
2 Light Candlestick
6½″ H. x 7″ W.

No. 115-123
2 Light Candelabra
6¼″ H. x 8¼″ W.

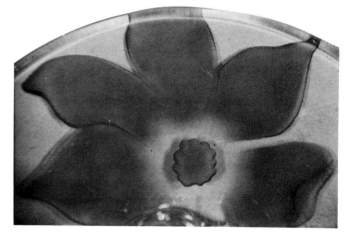

1

2

3

4

5

6

7

8

No. 115
3 Light Candlestick
Height 5″   Width 8½″

No. 115
3 Light Candelabrum W/Cut Prisms
2 Bobeches
Height 6″   Width 9½″

No. 115
2 Light Epergne Candlestick
W/Vase
Height 9½″   Width 8½″

No. 115
2 Light Epergne Candelabrum
W/Vase   W/Cut Prisms
Height 9½″   Width 9½″

No. 41
5 in. 2 Light Candelabrum
W/Cut Prisms
Height 6¾"   Width 7½"

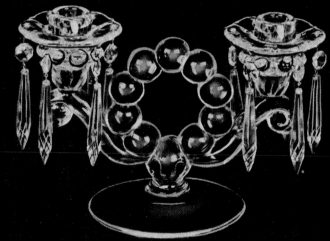

No. 301
2 Light Candelabrum
W/Cut Prisms
Height 7"   Width 10"

No. 14
3 Light Candelabrum
W/Prisms—3 Bobesches
Height 8"   Width 10"

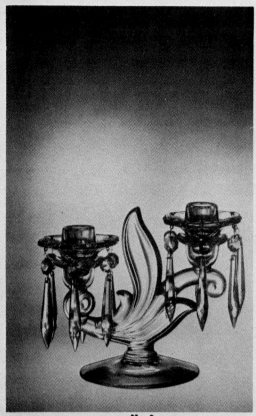

No. 3
2 Light Candelabra W/Cut Prisms
Height 7"   Width 7"

No. 2
2 Light Candelabra W/Cut Prisms
Height 9½"   Width 7½"

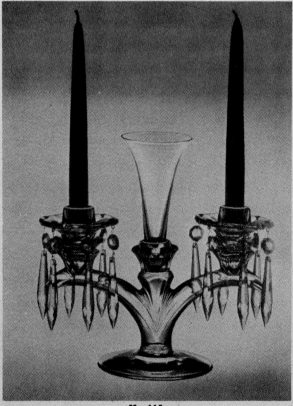

No. 115
2 Light Epergne Candelabra W/Vase
W/Cut Prisms—2 Bobesches
Height 9"   Width 9"

No. 115
3 Light Candelabra W/Cut Prisms
2 Bobesches
Height 6"   Width 9"

No. 1-B-41
3 Light Candelabrum W/Cut Prisms
Height 10"   Width 13"
2 Bobeches

No. 1-41
1 Light Candelabrum W/Cut Prisms
Height 10"

No. 1-41
1 Light Hurricane Lamp
Candelabrum W/Prisms
Height 15"

No. 1-C-41
3 Light Candelabrum W/Cut Prisms
Height 16"   Width 13"
3 Bobeches

120/5

120/6

120/7

120/8

220/3

220/

220/5

220/6

1&5.   No. 232, Circa 1925, 8½" high.
Colors: velva rose shown. Other known colors are florentine (stretch) and marigold. Current value, $30.00 - 35.00

2,3,4.   No. 950, Circa 1936-1939.
3-Piece Console Set, Satin Poinsettia etching, Cornucopia candlesticks, other etchings used were "San-Toy" and "Silver Tone". The set may also be found with a No. 1663 centerpiece bowl and was sold as No. 950/1663 - 3 Piece Console Set. Colors: crystal (satin) shown. Other known colors are royal blue, miny rose, amber and azure blue (pale blue stretch glass). Current value $26.00 - 32.00

6.   No. 318, Circa 1926-1980, 2" high.
Sold as a Console Set No. 1502 in 1927. No. 1502 was known as Diamond Optic Line. Colors were plain rose, plain green and orchid. In 1933 issued as No. 100. was sold with 9" octagon bowl as No. 318 Console Set. Made in ruby and jade green. Again in 1980, issued as No. 7572VR in velva rose (a new generation of iridized stretch glass). Colors: cameo (shown), other known color, not listed above, is tangerine. Current value, $18.00 - 20.00

7.   No. 1623, Dolphin, Circa 1928-1937, 3½" high.
May be found with spiral-optic base or plain base; the number is the same. Colors: topaz (shown), velva rose, green, florentine green, jade green, ruby, aquamarine, rose, crystal with inta-base (flower). Current value, $35.00 - 40.00

8.   Fenton "Shelf" Sign, Circa 1978.
Made for Fenton Art Glass Collectors of America (see society listings in front of book). No value placed

9.   No. 389, Hobnail, Circa 1941-1969, 4½" high.
Sold in 1942-43 as No. 389, 3 Piece Console Set with No. 389 9" Double Crimped Bowl. Reissued in 1953 as Pattern No. 3974; was still made in 1969. Colors: topaz opalescent (shown), turquoise, crystal opalescent, blue opalescent and french opalescent. Current value, $24.00 - 26.00

10.   No. 315, Circa 1925, 3½" high.
Colors: Amber (shown), Chinese yellow. Current value, $28.00 - 32.00

11,12,13.   No. 752, Console Set, Circa 1951-1952.
Colors: milk glass (shown), emerald green. Current value, items 11 and 13, $15.00 - 18.00, current value item 12, $35.00 - 40.00

1

2

3

4

5

6

7

8

9

10

11

12

13

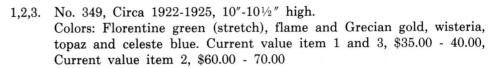

Our oldest, most popular pattern . . .

From a recent Fenton brochure.

1,2,3. No. 349, Circa 1922-1925, 10″-10½″ high.
Colors: Florentine green (stretch), flame and Grecian gold, wisteria, topaz and celeste blue. Current value item 1 and 3, $35.00 - 40.00, Current value item 2, $60.00 - 70.00

4&6. No. 696, Northwood, Circa 1924, 10″ high & 8½″ high.
Shown for comparison. Note that the Northwood Candlestick is thicker in the base and stem and has a knob or ring rather than a flair-indentation at the stem and base. See Northwood Plate 41. Current value, $40.00 - 45.00.

5&11. No. 449, Circa 1922-1925, 8½″ high.
Colors: wisteria and crystal (shown), mandarin red, ruby (plain and stretch), celeste blue, jade yellow, turquoise, Florentine green, Grecian gold and ebony. (Elbony can also be found decorated.) Item 11 has an engraved cutting on the stem. From all records available, we find no listing for this article having been engraved. Therefore, we believe the engraving was not done at Fenton, but elsewhere. Current value item 5, $30.00 - 35.00. Current value item 11, $18.00 - 22.00.

7,8,10. No. 549, Circa 1923-26, 8″-8½″ high.
Two-tone combination shown, flame with royal blue base. Any two-tone combination is rare. Colors: flame royal blue (shown), marigold, topaz, flame, peking blue, and moonstone with ebony base. Current value item 7, $50.00 - 60.00. Current value item 8 and 10, $22.00 - 28.00.

9. No. 649, Circa 1923-1926, 10″-10½″ high.
Only difference between No. 549 and No. 649 is height. Shown is Grecian gold; candlestick with fairy lamp base (cup by Victrylite Candle Company; Oshkosh, WI, shade from A-A Imports of St. Louis). Grecian gold is sameshade as marigold, the finish is the difference (slight stretch). Other known colors are wisteria with Persian pearl base and Grecian gold with black (ebony) base. Current value $35.00 - 40.00.

Fenton

1

2

3

4

5

6

7

8

9

10

11

1. 1700RH, Christmas Holly Fairy Lamp, Circa 1976, 5½″ high.
   Crystal base, ruby shade, hand decorated, also made in custard, No. 7300CH. Current value, $18.00 - 20.00.

5. Reproduction (not Fenton).
   Base slightly smaller, but appears to be a direct copy. Shown for comparison. Current value, $8.00 - 10.00.

2,3,4. No. 6, Swan Console Set, Circa 1938, 6½″ high.
   Consists of: 2 No. 6 Swan Candlesticks, 1 No. 6 Swan Bowl (square). The candlestick can be found with a "bell" shaped base. Candlesticks shown are "flat" at the base. The No. 6 Swan Bowl can also be found with one swan's head down, one up, known as a "tulip" bowl. Colors: satin crystal (shown), rose, amethyst and amber. A very rare color in opalescent blue can be found. Any other opalescent colors should be considered rare also. Current value items 2 and 4, $30.00 - 35.00. Current value item 3, $45.00 - 50.00.

6,7,9,10. No. 848, Circa 1932, 2″ high.
   Multi-colors shown with several variants in the dish part of the candleholder (listed as candleholder rather than candlestick). Typical "Fenton Foot" of the 1930's. This foot or leg was used on many items. Colors shown are crystal, royal blue, green and ruby. Other known colors are jade and black (ebony). Current value items 6 and 9, $16.00 - 20.00. Current value item 7, $25.00 - 30.00. Current value item 10, $20.00 - 22.00.

8. No. 8409 VE, Currier and Ives Fairy Lamp (Light vase), Circa 1979. With candle insert, colors: frosted crystal (shown), antique blue and antique brown. Current value, $20.00 - 24.00.

11&12. No. 1621, Dolphin-Handle-Dish Candlestick, Circa 1928-1936.
   Date established based on other articles made in this pattern such as No. 1521 dishes and bowls. Shown is flat dish and flat dish with flared sides. Colors: aquamarine blue, rose, jade and green. Current values, $30.00 - 32.00.

13. No. 249, Circa 1921-1937, 6″ high.
   Special treatment: San Toy Etching in 1936, Ruby Stretch in 1921, Snow Fern etching in 1937, Celeste Blue Stretch in 1921. Colors: ruby (shown), celeste blue, marigold, and Grecian gold. Current value, $30.00 - 34.00.

14. Fenton? Some question exists that this is a Fenton candlestick.
   The jade color is very close to Fenton jade, however, if it is not a Fenton item, it's got to be Northwood. Do not confuse the basic design with Fenton No. 315. The socket on this one is panelled, the Fenton No. 315 is not. Current value, $24.00 - 26.00.

Milk glass from a recent Fenton brochure.

1

2

3

4

5

6

7

8

9

10

11

12

13

14

Fostoria GLASSWARE

CANDELABRAS
CANDLESTICKS AND
CANDLE LIGHTING GOODS

U Drop Prism

Spearhead Prism

No. 21. Lustre Candlestick
With Spearhead Prisms
Height 12½ in. Diameter of Base 5½ in

Candleholder

Bobache

No. 17. 5-Light Candelabra
With U Drop Prisms
Height 23 inches. Spread 15 inches
Diameter of Base 8 inches

No. 22. 2-Light Candelabra
With U Drop Prisms
Height 20 inches. Spread 15 inches
Diameter of Base 6½ inches

No. 1103. Lustre
Height 14½ inches

No. 1103. Lustre
Height 22½ inches

1&3. No. 1103, Luster, Circa 1901-1938, 14½″ high.
This candlestick was also known as No. 2412 "Queen Ann" Design which was introduced in 1926, and discontinued in 1929. It was reintroduced in 1938 as "Colony" Pattern. The Colony Pattern was still made after 1938, but we have found no record indicating that No. 1103 Luster continued with the line. Oddly enough, this is the only pair (or single) that we have ever found for sale. Colors: crystal (shown), the "Queen Ann" catalog (years 1926-29), indicated that the stems were made in amber, blue, green and crystal. The prisms, candleholder (socket) and bobeche were made in crystal only. To find this item in color would be very rare. Was also made 18½″ high. Current value, $100.00 - 125.00.

2. No. 1, Candelabra 4-Light, Circa 1901-1924, 21″ high - 12″ spread.
This item can be found 24″ high (center socket, socket stem 3″ higher) and is listed as No. 2 Candelabra. The No. 1 Candelabra was also furnished with an epergne (bud vase to replace the center socket. The 1901 date was used because we have a 1901 catalog that lists it. Going through the files at Fostoria, we found no catalog before this date. However, as this item was No. 1 & No. 2, we believe that it was one of the first items made, therefore, it could have been made as early as 1887. Made only in crystal. Current value, $350.00 - 400.00.

4. Baccarat (Mold-Marked), 7½″ high.
Shown for comparison. We do not know the date that the Baccarat Candlestick was made, therefore, we do not know who copied who! We have not seen a Baccarat Twist larger than the one shown, and have not seen it in any colors. Current value, $75.00 - 100.00.

5. No. 4, Lustre (fixed No. 4 bobeche-applied) Circa 1901-1924, 10″ high.
In 1938 No. 4 Lustre was issued as "Colony" Pattern. A lot of the "Twist" patterns were used for the "Queen Ann" Design. We are not aware that this item was ever issued for it. Believed to be made only in crystal. Current value, $40.00 - 45.00.

No. 4. Lustre Candlestick
With U Drop Prisms
Height 10 in. Diameter of Base 5 in.

No. 1. 4-Light Candelabra
With U Drop Prisms
Height 21 inches. Spread 12 inches
Diameter of Base 6 inches

No. 4
Bobache and U Drop Prisms
can be used on any candlestick

No. 112. 9-inch

No. 1103. 9½-inch

6. Fostoria "Shelf Sign" (Plastic).
Given to us by the factory. No value placed.

7. No. 112 with No. 4 Bobeche and 10 Spearhead prisms.
For information, see item 8 below. Current value, $35.00 - 40.00.

8. No. 112, Circa 1901-1924, 9″ high.
This basic candlestick was used for No. 4 Lustre (item 5 above), therefore we believe that it was issued before 1901. We have no record that lists it past 1924, even though the No. 4 Lustre was produced in 1938. Made only in crystal. Current value, $30.00 - 32.00.

9. No. 2412, Lustre, Circa 1938-1972, 7½″ high.
Colony Pattern with 8 "U" prisms. We find no record past 1972. Colors: crystal shown. A 1939 catalog specified that customers should "see price list for colors". We have never seen it in color. Current value, $32.00 - 35.00.

10. Mckee "Ray", 8″ high.
Shown for comparison. Notice the color difference in the crystal. The Mckee "Ray" most likely has Selenium (de-colorizing agent) in it and has been discolored by the sun. Current value, $30.00 - 34.00.

11. Spear-Head 2-light, Circa 1940-1950, 6″ high.
We are not aware of any other colors. Current value, $22.00 - 28.00.

12. No. 1103, Circa 1906-1924, 9½″ high.
We are not aware of any other colors. Do not confuse this candlestick with the No. 1103 Lustre (item 1 & 3 above). The socket and base are different. Yet they are shown in a 1924 catalog with the same pattern number. Current value, $34.00 - 36.00.

No. 13. 5-Light Candelabra
With U Drop Prisms
Height 18 inches. Spread 15 inches

Fostoria
GLASSWARE

1

2

3

Fostoria

4

5

6

7

8

9

10

11

12

No. 161. 7-inch

No. 5A. 2-Light Candelabra
With U Drop Prisms
Height 16 inches. Spread 14 inches
Diameter of Base 6 inches

No. 7. 5-Light Candelabra
With U Drop Prisms
Height 23 inches. Spread 15 inches
Diameter of Base 7 inches

No. 15. 2-Light Candelabra
With U Drop Prisms
Height 13 inches. Spread 14 inches
Diameter of Base 7 inches

1&3.   No. 2324, Tall, Circa 1924-1929, 12″ high.
Patent no. 68657, also made 2″, 4″, 6″ & 9″ high (4″ shown below, items 8, 9, 11, 12). Colors: green (shown), crystal, amber, blue, and orchid (orchid not made in 12″). Current value, $42.00 - 46.00.

2.   No. 2415, Combination Bowl-Firenze, Circa 1929-1932.
Firenze (topaz with gold rim) very rare. Firenze was only used for this item for 2 years, 1931 & 1932. The etching shown is "Verona" Design, Plate Etching No. 281. The design and etching can also be found in crystal, rose and green. We are not sure that 1929 is the first year that the combination bowl was made. We do know that it was also used for the "Trojan" Design which was introduced in 1929, but lived a long life into 1944. Current value, $45.00 - 50.00.

4,5,6,7.   No. 2496 Line-Baroque Pattern
Color & life span:

Color	Description	Years
Crystal		1935-1966
Azure	Slight greenish-blue tint	1936-1944
Topaz	Slight yellow tint	1936-1938
Gold tint	Canary yellow (heavy)	1938-1944
Ruby	Red (rare color)	1936-1939

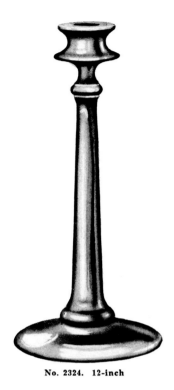

No. 2324. 12-inch

No. 2324. 12-inch
Etched

No. 2324. 9-inch

No. 2324. 9-inch
Etched

No. 2324. 4-inch

Items Shown:

4. Azure - 4″ high.
   This candlestick can be found in crystal with etched designs in Meadow Rose and Beacon. Current value, $18.00 - 20.00.

5. Crystal-Duo Candlestick, 4½″ high, 8″ spread.
   Table settings using this candlestick were Corsage, Navarre and Beacon. Current value, $20.00 - 22.00.

6. Gold Tint-Trindle Candlestick, 6″ high, 8¼″ spread.
   Table settings using this candlestick were Corsage, Navarre, Rambler, Watercress and Beacon. Current value, $25.00 - 30.00. Items 5 & 6 may also be found in Silver Mist (Crystal with a soft, smooth matte finish) A difficult item to find. Introduced in 1934, discontinued in 1940.

7. Crystal - 5½″ high.
   Etching: Corsage Design-Plate Etching #325, introduced in 1935, discontinued in 1966, other table settings using this candlestick were Navarre, Meadow Rose, Cyrene, Beacon, Federal and Tulip. Current value, $16.00 - 18.00.

8,9,10,11,12. No. 2324, Circa 1924-1933, 4″ high.
   These items are shown together to allow a color comparison and to show the unusual treatment of the bowl base (a No. 2324 candlestick applied to the bowl top).

No. 2324. 4-inch
Etched

8. No. 2324 Gold Tint (not listed in colors). Cutting (engraving) not believed to be Fostoria. Current value, $12.00 - 14.00.

9,10,11. No. 2324 Console Set (bowl No. unknown) amber.
   Current value, $12.00 - 16.00.

12. No. 2324 Orchid with gold decoration.
   Current value, $12.00 - 14.00. Other colors not shown: rose, ebony, azure, green, crystal and blue.
   Etch patterns used with No. 2324 -
   Grape Design, brocade etching No. 287 circa 1927-1930. Made in blue and orchid 1927-1929, green 1927-1939. Used with No. 2329 bowl as console set.
   "Cupid" Pattern, plate etching No. 288 (very rare) circa 1927-1929. Made in amber, blue, green and ebony.
   "Paradise" Pattern, (issued also as "Victoria", decoration No. 71,) plate etching No. 289. circa 1927-1930. Made in green and orchid. Colors: iridescent and mother-of-pearl. We have never seen either color in this pattern.
   Cut pattern used with No. 2324 -
   "Arbor" cutting No. 184 circa 1926-1928 made in amber, blue and green.
   "Berry" cutting No. 188 circa 1928-1929 made in green and rose (dawn).
   "Kingsley" cutting No. 192 - polished circa 1929-1930. Made in rose and azure.

No. 2056. 7¼-inch

314

319

331

1,2,3. Heirloom Console Set, circa 1959-1962.
Consists of: No. 2183/311 Flora Candle (made only 1959-1962) No. 1515/279 16″ Oval Centerpiece (made 1959-1970) Colors: blue (shown), green, opal, pink, yellow, bittersweet (orange); centerpiece. Current value, $32.00 - 38.00.

AMERICAN PATTERN

4&6. No. 2056½/331 Twin circa 1975, 5½ high.
We are not sure of the exact date that the No. 331-Twin was introduced. We do have a 1976 catalog which still lists it. Current value, $18.00 - 20.00.

5. No. 2056, Duo, circa 1939-1960, 6½″ high.
This item is listed in a 1939 catalog as No. 2056 2-light Candelabra; using 16 "U" drop prisms on a No. 2527 bobeche. Current value, $18.00 - 20.00.

7,8,9. Boudoir Set, circa 1915-1927.
Consists of: 2 No. 2056½ 7¼″ candlesticks, 2 No. 2056½ cologne bottles, 1 No. 2056 square puff and cover and 1 No. 2056½ 10″ comb and brush tray. Current value, $30.00 - 45.00.

Boudoir sets were also solid with a No. 2056 candlestick, quart jug (water pitcher), tumbler (8 ounce capacity), and a match box. We have yet to find a No. 2056 candlestick for sale. All glass houses have one pattern which remains in production year after year, is accepted by customers and ends up being accepted by their grandchildren. This is the case of No. 2056 American Pattern. It was introduced in 1915, and is still made today. We do not have all of the dates that the various candlesticks were issued in this pattern, but we have listed what has been available to us. The only candlesticks not shown are No. 314 3″ and No. 319, 6″. Further research revealed that No. 314 (re-issued in the 1970's) was, in fact, first issued in 1936 and discontinued in 1944. Also, the No. 2056 was made in azure and gold tint from 1938-1940. We have yet to see an American Pattern in color.

1,2,3. No. 2362, Console Set, circa 1926-1931.
Consists of: 2 No. 2362 candlestick, 3″ high. Can be found 9″ high. 1 No. 2292 vase. Colors: green (shown), crystal (see items 9, 10 and 11 below), amber, blue and orchid. Current value, $12.00 - 16.00.

4. No. 1513, No Handle, circa 1920-1925, 2½″ high.
Also found as No. 1513 with handle. We are not aware of any colors except crystal. Current value, $8.00 - 12.00

5. No. 2527, 2-light candelabra, circa 1936-1960.
Was made to use No. 2527 bobeches with 16 "U" drop prisms. Table settings using this candlestick were: "Corsage" (1935-1960), "Heirloom" (1935-1939), "Society" (1935-1938), "Bouquet" (1935-1939), and "Laurel" (1938-1960). Colors: crystal shown. Catalog indicated that it was introduced in colors. We believe these colors to be azure and gold tint. We have not seen this item other than in crystal. Current value, $14.00 - 16.00.

No. 1513. No Handle

No. 1513. Handled

[271] FINE CRYSTAL, hand blown, hand cut, and polished in a graceful floral design: COLONIAL SUGAR and CREAMER, set - $8; CANDELABRA with prisms, 8″ high, 7″ span - $20 the pair; ICEPAIL 5″ dia, 5¾″ high - $7.50, 6″ dia, 7″ high - $8.50; FRUIT BOWL 12¼″ dia, 3½″ deep - $13; same 14″ dia, 4½″ deep - $22

6. No. 2395½, circa 1928-1952, 5″ high.
Introduced in 1928 in the following colors: rose, azure, green, amber, topaz, ebony and crystal. This candlestick was used mostly for "June" design, plate etching No. 279 (shown). Colors for "June" design were as follows: rose (dawn), azure, green (1928-1944), topaz (shown) (1929-1938) and gold tint (1938-1944). The "June" design No. 2395½ was not made in crystal. One other table setting that used this candlestick was "fuchia" (1931-1944). Current value, $10.00 - 18.00.

7. No. 2470½, No. 2470 line, circa 1931-1944 5½″ high.
These dates are contrary to one catalog listing, which indicated it was introduced in 1933 and discontinued in 1942. A number of table settings using No. 2470½ were introduced in 1931 and discontinued in 1957. Table settings using this candlestick were: "Manor" (1931-1944), "Fuchsia" (1931-1944), "Florentine" (1931-1944), "Morning glory" (1931-1944), "Chateau" (1933-1940), "Midnight rose" (1933-1957) and "Springtime" (1933-1944). Colors: crystal (shown). Colors were made in the following years; rose and green (1933-1942), wisteria and topaz (1933-1938), gold tint (1938-1942). Possible can be found in ruby (1935-1939), regal blue, burgandy, and empire green (1933-1942). Current value, $8.00 - 12.00.

8&12. No. 2535, circa 1935-1960, 5½ high.
Again these dates are contrary to one catalog listing which indicated it was introduced in 1936 and discontinued in 1944. Colors were produced but we do not have a listing. Table settings using this candlestick were: "Daisy" (1935-1944), "Corsage" (1935-1960), "Gossamer" (1935-1940) and "Ivy" (1935-1944). Item 12 shown with a No. 122 bobeche (circa 1901). Current value, $10.00 - 16.00.

9,10,11. No. 2362, Console Set.
See information item 1, 2, & 3 above. This set shown is a typical cut set. The bowl is No. 2342. The cutting is "Louisa", cutting No. 168 (sorry that it did not photograph better). Etched patterns were as follows: "Grape" introduced 1927, discontinued 1930. Colors: blue and orchid 1927-29, green 1927-1930. "Paradise" introduced 1927, discontinued 1930. Colors: green and orchid. Also presented as "Victoria", decoration No. 71 "Victoria" made in mother of pearl and iridescent. Current Value, $10.00 - 16.00.

No. 1204. 8½-inch

No. 1204. 8½-inch
Deep Etched "D"

No. 2246. 8¼-inch
Deep Etched

No. 1218. 8-inch
Deep Etched "A"

No. 2269. 6-inch
Deep Etched

No. 2244. 6-inch
Deep Etched

No. 2268. 6-inch
Deep Etched

5-inch Christmas Candle

No. 19.   12-inch

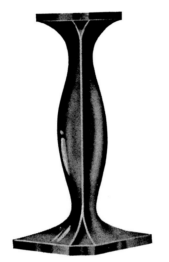

No. 1205.   8-inch

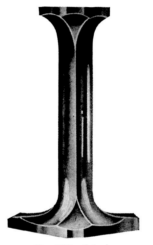

No. 1218.   8-inch

No. 2311.   7-inch

No. 1490.   8-inch

No. 1639.   8-inch

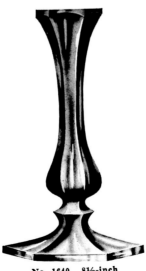

No. 1640.   8½-inch

No. 1642.   8-inch

No. 2247.   8½-inch

Fostoria GLASSWARE

No. 1081.   8-inch

1. No. 1081, circa 1920-1935, 8″ high.
    Made only in crystal. Current value, $28.00 - 32.00.

2,3&4. No. 2297, Console Set, circa 1924-1928.
    Consists of: 2 No. 2297 7″ high candlestick, 1 No. 2297 10½″ deep bowl - "C" rolled edge. Colors: blue shown. Other known colors are crystal, amber, canary and green. Current value, $22.00 - 26.00.

5. No. 1485 (Plain), circa 1915-1925, 8″ high.
    Can be found 11″ high. One catalog lists the years as above, another lists the years 1920-1925. Current value, $16.00 - 18.00.

6. No. 1513, No Handle.
    See details on Plate 19, item 4. Current value, $8.00 - 12.00.

7&9. No. 2298, age unknown, 3″ high.
    Only record we have seen shows No. 2298 used with plate etching No. 288, "Cupid" Pattern which was introduced in 1927 and discontinued 1929. Colors: topaz (shown), amber, blue, green, and ebony. Current value, $14.00 - 18.00.

8. Fostoria "Shelf" Sign.
    No value placed.

10. No. 1666, Handled, circa 1920-1925.
    Made only in crystal. Current value, $12.00 - 16.00.

11. No. 2436, Lustre, circa 1930-1935, 9″ high.
    Shown with "U" drop prisms. Was also sold with tear-drop prisms. Colors: topaz base and stem - crystal top (shown), rose, green amber, crystal, and ebony. Current value, $40.00 - 45.00.

12&14. No. 2372, "Spiral Optic" (S/O), circa 1926-1931.
    Dates based on other "Spiral Optic" items. Colors: amber (shown), blue, green, and crystal. Current value, $10.00 - 12.00.

13. Life-Saver, age unknown (Believed to be 1930-1935.) 6″ high.
    We have not shown many candlesticks that we do not have records showing their shape, size etc. This one is the exception. We conferred with many knowledgeable people before listing this item as Fostoria. The color is topaz. Current value, $15.00 - 18.00.

15. No. 2245, circa 1924-1928, 8″ high.
    Also made 6″ high and used for deep etched patterns. Colors: amber (shown), canary, green, blue, and crystal. Current value, $25.00 - 30.00.

No. 2297.   7-inch   No. 2299.   5-inch

No. 1485.   8-inch
Cut 160

No. 1485.   8-inch
Deep Etched "B"

No. 1666.   Handled

No. 2245.   8¼-inch
Deep Etched

No. 2245.   6-inch
Deep Etched

1

2

3

4

5

6

7

8

9

10

11

12

13

14

15

Fostoria
GLASS WARE

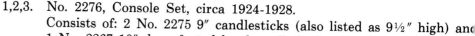

No. 2275. 7-inch

No. 2275. 9-inch
Deep Etched

1,2,3. No. 2276, Console Set, circa 1924-1928.
Consists of: 2 No. 2275 9″ candlesticks (also listed as 9½″ high) and 1 No. 2267 10″ deep footed bowl - rolled edge (bowl sitting on ebony bowl base used for photography only, not part of set). Colors: amber with white ringed decoration (shown), canary, green and blue. This set was also used for "Virginia" blown ware, deep etched No. 267. We do not understand the term "Blown Ware" associated with this molded candlestick. The No. 2275 candlestick was used for other etched patterns. Current value, $18.00 - 24.00.

4. No. 1842, circa 1920-1925, 8½ high.
Made only in crystal. (Etching colored for photography on all candlesticks except items 7 and 10). Current value, $32.00 - 36.00.

5. No. 1856, "Cupid" etched, circa 1920-1925, 8″ high.
Made only in crystal (Color added in etching for photographing). Current value, $40.00 - 48.00.

6. No. 1639, Etched "D", circa 1915-1925, 8″ high.
Two references list this item with a conflict of dates produced. One (as indicated) 1915-1925, another indicated the date as 1920-1925. Made only in crystal (Color added in etching for photographing). Current value, $40.00 - 46.00.

7&10. No. 1490, Etched C-2 gold filled etching, circa 1920-1925, 8″ high.
Made only in crystal. Current value, $36.00 - 40.00.

8. Springtime, circa 1925-1930, 8″ high.
Springtime is a name that we have given this candlestick. We can find no record of it being Fostoria, or from another glass maker. We have attributed it to Fostoria because of its basic makeup - the etching, glass and style. We would not normally show it, but, we felt strongly that it is Fostoria. Current value, $40.00 - 46.00.

9. No. 1964, etched, circa 1920-1925, 9″ high.
Made only in crystal (Color added in etching for photographing). Current value, $44.00 - 50.00.

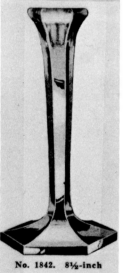

No. 1842. 8½-inch

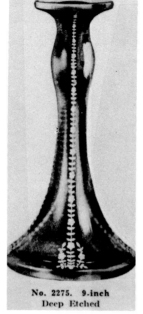

No. 1856. 8-inch
Deep Etched

No. 1490. 8-inch
Deep Etched C-2

No. 1490. 8-inch
Cut 162

No. 1964. 9-inch
Deep Etched

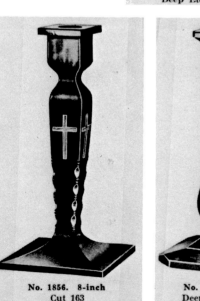

No. 1856. 8-inch
Cut 163

No. 1639. 8-inch
Deep Etched "D"

1

2

3

4

5

6

7

8

9

10

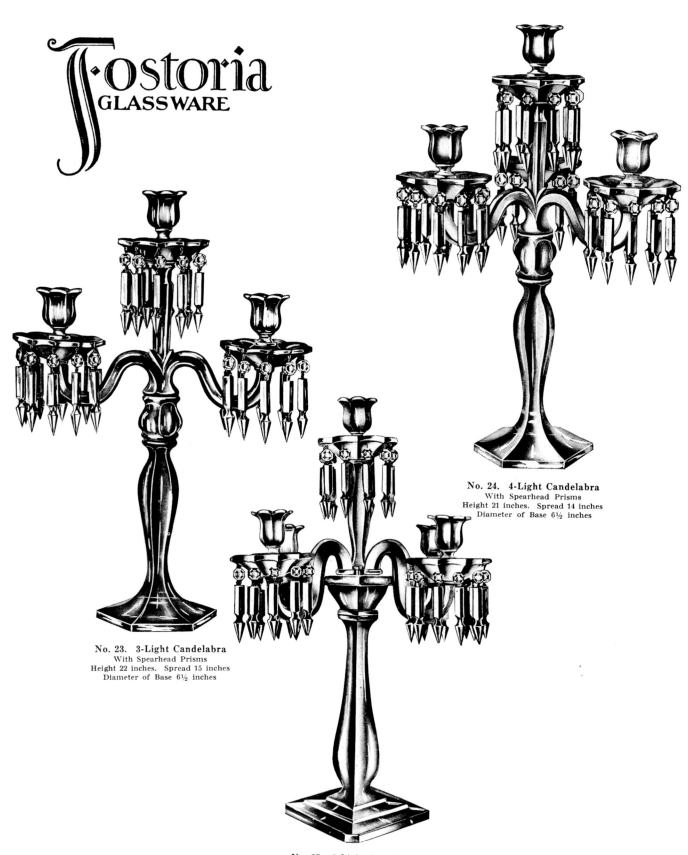

Fostoria GLASSWARE

No. 24. 4-Light Candelabra
With Spearhead Prisms
Height 21 inches. Spread 14 inches
Diameter of Base 6½ inches

No. 23. 3-Light Candelabra
With Spearhead Prisms
Height 22 inches. Spread 15 inches
Diameter of Base 6½ inches

No. 25. 5-Light Candelabra
With Spearhead Prisms
Height 24 inches. Spread 18 inches
Diameter of Base 8½ inches

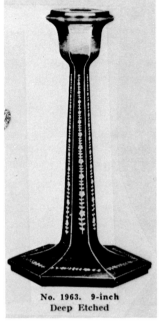

No. 1963. 9-inch
Deep Etched

1. No. 1963, circa 1920-1925, 9″ high.
This item is shown for shape only. To untangle the question of the manufacturer at this time has become almost impossible. We believe this candlestick to be Fostoria. The only true way to tell it to have one with "small flower" deep etched on the stem. We have found no indication of No. 1963 being issued plain. Therefore, without the "deep etch", it will most likely be New Martinsville No. 10-21 or Paden City No. 115. We are not aware that the Fostoria candlestick was made in any color other than crystal. Current value, $26.00 - 30.00.

2. No. 2636, Plume Duo, circa 1953, 9½″ high.
Can also be found in a single light. Made only in crystal. Current value, $32.00 - 36.00.

3. No. 2601, Lyre Duo, circa 1941-1953, 8″ high.
This is a single-light lyre candlestick but it was not manufactured by Fostoria. We have not identified the single-light lyre. Fostoria lyre made only in crystal. Current value, $28.00 - 32.00.

4. No. 2394, Dish Candlestick, circa 1928-1952, 2″ high.
Based on years that "June" Design was produced. We have no introduction date on all of the colors that were produced, therefore, we can only list the patterns (designs) that used this article.
Colors and Patterns: green shown.
"June" - rose (dawn), azure, green. 1928-1944
topaz 1929-1938
gold tint 1938-1944
crystal 1928-1952
"Oak leaf" - rose (dawn), green 1928-1931
ebony 1929-1931
"Orleans" - azure, topaz 1929-1930
"Manor" - crystal 1931-1944
green 1931-1935
topaz 1931-1938
"Berry" (cutting) - green, rose (dawn) 1928-1929
"Chatteris" (polished cutting No. 197) - interesting note: catalog indicated that it was made in solid Crystal - Regular Optic.
"Acanthus" - green, amber 1931-1933

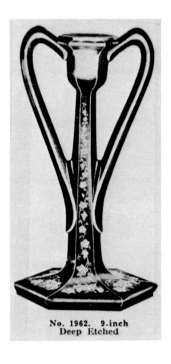

No. 1962. 9-inch
Deep Etched

◄ No. 1962 shows the "handled" version of the No. 1963. We have never seen a No. 1962.

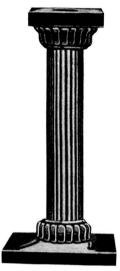

No. 1064.   8-inch

No. 2279.   Candleholder and
Bobache Combined
Diameter 4½ inches
This can be used on any
candlestick

5. Fostoria "shelf" Advertising Sign, circa 1981.
Current value, NVP.

6. No. 2395, age unknown, 3″ high.
Patterns and colors: "Oak Leaf" - rose (dawn), green, crystal 1928-1931
ebony 1929-1931. Amber shown. Total issued colors unknown. Current
value, $8.00 - 10.00.

7. No. 1064, Column, circa 1902-1925, 8″ high.
Fostoria records indicate that although this is a candlestick, it was also
sold as a shelf support for use in store displays and show windows.
Made only in crystal. Current value, $24.00 - 34.00.

8&10. No. 2545, "Flame" Lustre, circa 1937-1972, 7½″ high.
Dates based on "Navarre" Design which used No. 2545 as an item in
the table setting. Shown with 8 cut spearhead prisms (each). Was
originally sold with "U" drop prisms.
Patterns and colors:
 "Lido" Design shown. Plate etching No. 329 crystal 1937-1955.
 azure 1938-1943 (only color found).
 No. 2545 4½″ high. Colors unknown.
 No. 2545 "Flame" Duo, 6¾″ high. Azure and gold tint 1936-1944.
 No. 2545 2-light "Flame" Candelabra, 12 "B" prisms and No.
 25 45 bobeche. Azure and gold tint 1936-1944.
Current value, $22.00 - 26.00.

9. No. 2443, circa 1931-1944, 4″ high.
Total use of colors unknown. Topaz shown with heavy etching and
threading under the gold incrusted base.
Known patterns and colors:
 "Manor" - crystal 1931-1944, green 1931-1935, topaz 1931-1938.
 "Wildflower" - green and amber 1931-1933.
Current value, $10.00 - 12.00

11. No. CODE CA-11, item 327 "Sandwich", introduced 1976, 9″ high.
We are not aware of any other color. Current value, $28.00 - 32.00.

1

2

3

4

5

6

7

8

9

10

11

Fostoria GLASSWARE

1. No. 2630, Century Trindle, circa 1956-1981, 7¾" high. Pattern Code CEO1, item 336, made only in crystal. Current value, $20.00 - 26.00.

2. No. CA12/337, Candelabra, circa 1975-1980, 12" high, 14½" spread

Consists of:
1 CA12/336 3-light candlestick
3 CA12/132 bobeches
30 TRO2/981 spearhead prisms

Made only in crystal. Current value, $350.00 - 375.00.

3. No. 2630, Century Duo, circa 1956-1981, 7" high. Pattern Code CEO1, item 332, made only in crystal. Current value, $16.00 - 18.00.

4,5,6,7. No. 1372, Line Coin Glass, circa 1976-1981

4. No. 381, 4" high. Ruby (CO-05)* This item was first issued as a "footed cigarette urn". Current value, $14.00 - 16.00.

5 & 6 No. 326, 8" high. Green (CO-04) and ruby (CO-05). Current value, $28.00 - 30.00.

7. No. 316, 4½" high. Ruby (CO-05)

Other known colors are: crystal (CO-01), blue (CO-03) and amber (CO-02). Current value, $12.00 - 14.00.

*Color code

8 & 12. No. 2433, circa 1930-1935, 3" high.

Colors: green base with crystal top (shown), amber, ebony base with crystal top, crystal base with rose top, and azure base with topaz top. Patterns and colors: "Minuet" - green, topaz, topaz top with crystal base, crystal with green base. 1930-1934. "Wildflower" - green and amber. 1931-1933. Current value, $18.00 - 20.00.

9,10,11. Avon by Fostoria, circa 1978-1981.

We do not have numbers or information for these items, but felt that it was important to show representatives of candlesticks by Fostoria, made for Avon. Current value, $10.00 - 16.00.

Interesting item, 9 & 10. Same candlestick turned upside down. You be the one to choose which is up and which is down . . . (candle dish in item 9 came as shown).

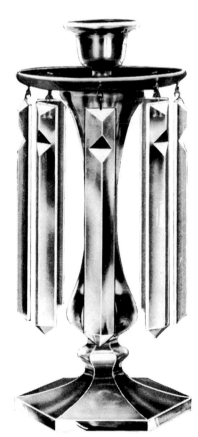

No. 1640. 11½-inch Lustre
With Fostoria 6-inch Prisms

No. 1965. 8-inch
Deep Etched

No. 1965. 8-inch
Cut 164

No. 2244. 8-inch
Deep Etched

Fostoria
GLASSWARE

1

2

3

4

5

6

7

8

9

10

11

12

BETTER HOMES & GARDENS
MAY, 1940

GOOD HOUSEKEEPING
DEC., 1924

BETTER HOMES & GARDENS
MAY, 1940

Heisey

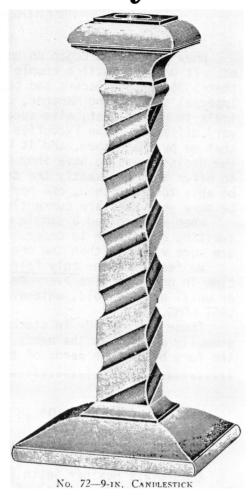

No. 72—9-in. Candlestick

We have been allowed by Heisey Collectors of America, Inc., to reprint the catalog cut above. We have this item but were unable to photograph it as it is on loan to the National Heisey Glass Museum, Newark, Ohio. It is not the rarest of candlesticks but it is very difficult to find. We believe it was made in crystal only.

1&3. No. 1469, Ridgeleigh Candle Vase, circa 1937-1940, 6″ high. Colors: sahara and zircon (shown), crystal. Current value, $65.00 - 80.00.

2. No. 301, Three Light Candelabrum, circa 1929-1953, 14½″ high, 13″ wide spread

Consists of:
1 No. 301 three light base
1 No. 300 three light arm
3 No. 300 bobeches'
3 No. 300 candleholders (sockets)
1 No. 51 ferrule (used to hold arm in base)
3 No. 54 ferrules (used to hold sockets to arm
30 "A" prisms (can also be found with "C" prisms)

Was also known as "Colonial Candelabrum", later changed to "Old Williamsburg". If found with beaded strands, known as "button strands" (bead of a "A" prism), it is a No. 301 Girondoles. We have revised the date of issue from original listing in one of our other books because of the color. The color sahara was not made before 1929. Also, the No. 301 base is a later vintage than we had based our other data on (1903 No. 300 Candelabrum). In 1958, Imperial reissued this item in crystal. It is still in production this date (1982). Colors: sahara shown. Other known colors are crystal, crystal with stiegel blue bobeches', stiegle blue base, and a combination of the two, stiegle blue base and bobeches' with crystal arms, and alexandrite base and bobeches with crystal arms. Current value, $350.00 - 400.00.

4&10. No. 116, Oak Leaf, circa 1927-1929, 3″ high. The design of this candlestick was submitted by T. C. Heisey for a patent on January 7, 1927 and was granted on December 6, 1927 (N o. D74,012). These candlesticks can be found with a matching bowl (No. 116 - floral) which has 4 oak leaves molded around the inside-upper portion of the bowl. Colors: Moongleam base - crystal socket with frosted oak leaves (shown), combination of crystal, hawthorne and flamingo (combination as shown). Current value, $22.00 - 26.00.

5. Blackout Lamp Base*, circa 1939-1942, 2½″ high. Base only shown. The item was sold with a cylinder-type shade (straight hurricane) as a set. We have not listed a number for this item, but an early Lariet advertisement included it as part of the Lariat Pattern No. 1540. Colors: made only in crystal (based on being a part of the Lariat line). Do not confuse this item with Imperial No. 110/80. The base and stem are very much alike, the shade-dish and socket are different. Current value, $40.00 - 45.00.

6. No. 30 Toy, circa 1913, 3″ high. You will encounter throughout the heisey plates, a number of small candlesticks referred to as "toy". These were original names used by Heisey. All listed will have a different number, but we did not wish to confuse you by calling other items by the same name without an explanation. Colors: only made in crystal. Current value, $25.00 - 30.00.

301
3-Lite Candelabra

7. Heisey "Cabachon" advertisement sign.
Believed to be issued in 1949. Color was added for photography. The sign is crystal with frosted letters. No value placed.

8. No. 31, Handled Toy, circa 1908-1937, 1½″ high.
This item has been reissued by Imperial in crystal (see Plate 33, item 5). The reissue date was early 1981. Colors: crystal (shown), sahara, moongleam, and flamingo. Current value, $20.00 - 25.00.

9. Duncan-Miller, 1½″ high.
Shown for comparison. It is very difficult to tell these two items apart (8 & 9) unless you are a Heisey or Duncan-Miller collector. The only obvious difference is in the placement (location) of the handle. The Heisey Handled Toy has the handle free and clear of the socket; (also most likely mold marked) the Duncan-Miller handle is part of (attached to) the socket. We are not aware that Duncan-Miller produced this item in any color other than crystal. Current value, $18.00 - 20.00.

11. No. 1504, 2-Light, circa 1940-1957.
1940 date was selected by us, the theory being that the basic candlestick used for Crystolite 1503 Pattern was introduced earlier and this item became a part of the Crystolite Line. This item is also known as No. 1504 Regency Double Candlestick. Later years, (Mid 1950's) it was advertised "to be used with Heisey Epergnettes". These were insert bobeches' and saucers (nappies) to hold flowers and a candle together. Colors: we are not aware of any color other than crystal. Current value, $25.00 - 30.00.

12. No. 134, Trident, circa 1932-1957, 5″ high.
If you wish to call one particular candlestick a "work-horse", this would have to be it. Used with many patterns, inter-mixed with such items as Empress, Waverly, etc., we find that it's difficult to tie-down the total usage. To touch on a few, we have found listing of 15 etchings (patterns) and 53 cuttings. We have not investigated the total number of Heisey cuttings, but this has to be a record for cutting use, for any product, by any glass manufacturer. Colors: flamingo (shown), moongleam, trial blue, sahara, alexandrite, tangerine and crystal. There are two-color combinations and if found should be considered rare (example: crystal with moongleam base). Current value, $50.00 - 60.00. This item was reissued by Imperial as No. 134/100 in crystal (1958-1971).

13. No. 1503, 3-light Crystolite, circa 1939-1957, 4″ high.
This candlestick was patented on March 20, 1939 as No. 115,400. Can be found with a center flower vase No. 4233. The flower vase in 5″ high and fits into the center socket. Colors: crystal shown. We know of no other colors. Current value, $20.00 - 25.00.

Heisey

Heisey

1. No. 1445, Grape, circa 1935-1944, 10″ high.
   Consists of: 1 No. 1445 candlestick, 1 No. 6 bobeche, and 12 "A" prisms. This pattern can be found in a 2-light which will not have bobeches'. This item was used with the following etchings Cuttings: etchings - No. 458 Olympiad and No. 600-601 Simplex (satin finish applied to the leaves and grapes only) Cuttings - Bacchus, Sweet Briar, Bonnie Briar, Continental, Manhatten, Singapore, Will-o-Wisp and Wakiki. Colors: crystal (shown), sahara, steigel blue, alexandrite, and it is believed that it may be found in flamingo and moongleam. Current value, $50.00 - 65.00.

2,3,4,5,6. No. 5, Colonial, circa 1903-1930.
   Designed by A. H. Heisey, Patent No. 37213, and was made in 7 different sizes. 5 are shown:
   2. No. 5, Toy, 5″ high, current values, $30.00 - 32.00.
   3. No. 5, Squat, 5½″ high. reissued by Imperial in 1980 (Imperial sticker on base). Current value $32.00 - 36.00.
   4. No. 5, 7″ high. Current value, $38.00 - 40.00.
   5. No. 5, 9″ high. Current value, $40.00 - 44.00.
   6. No. 5, 11″ high without shade. (bobeche and shade not believed to be Heisey). Current value, $50.00 - 55.00 without shade. Sizes not shown are 6″ and 8″ high.

   A 1910 price list indicated that these items were available with all surfaces cut (full cut). This essentially made it "cut glass" and was sold as such. Colors: made only in crystal. However a No. 5 1-light Candelabra Base (same basic shape) 7″ high was made for "one-turn" in moongleam in late 1925 and early 1926. There is a possibility that the moongleam item lived through 1927. The base, without the top, may be mis-identified as a No. 5 standard candlestick; otherwise, we would have omitted this information.

7. No. 99, Candle Block, circa 1929, 1″ high.
   Colors: flamingo (shown), crystal, and moongleam. Current value, $18.00 - 20.00.

8. No. 1509, Queen Ann - Plain, circa 1937-1957, 1½″ high.
   Can be found with 2 handles.

   Confusing facts - why not No. 1401 Empress? After studying known Empress items (Empress determined by color), the only detectable difference is panels and/or ridges in the Queen Ann glass, compared to the smooth surface on the inside of the dish of the Empress. Colors: it is an accepted opinion that Queen Ann was only made in crystal, however, Empress was made in color (see item 9 below). Current value, $20.00 - 25.00.

9. No. 1401, Empress, circa 1937-1957, 1½″ high.
   Colors: amber, shown (yet we find no listing for amber). Other known colors are alexanderite, flamingo, moongleam, sahara, steigel blue, tangerine and crystal. Late information indicates that this item may not be Heisey (based on size and color). Current value, $22.00 - 30.00.

10. No. 1550, Fish, circa 1941-1946, 3½″ high.
    Colors: we are not aware of any color other than crystal. Current value, $125.00 - 135.00.

Heisey

1   2   3   4   5   6

7   8   9   10

11   12   13   14

Heisey

11. No. 142, 3-Light Cascade, circa 1937-1957, 7″ high.
We feel that a lot more information on this candlestick other than what we have presented should be available. We have not been able to find any. This item was used for the following patterns: Heisey Rose, Minuet, Orchid. Reissued by Imperial (1958-1968) in crystal. Colors: we are not aware of any color except crystal. Current value, $30.00 - 34.00.

12. No. 22, circa 1908-1933, 7″ high. Also made in 9″ and 11″ high, the basic shape was used for a "Candle-Lamp" base.
No. 201 was used after No. 22 candlestick was discontinued. Colors: made in crystal only. Current value, $30.00 - 34.00.

13. No. 21, circa 1910-1930, 7″ high, also made 9″ high.
Design Patent No. 41590. In 1914, with the coming of electric lights, candlesticks were turned into lamps. No. 21 was one of many that Heisey used for this purpose. An early advertisement stated "A new and wonderful epoch in the evolution of ye old colonial candle stick". This item was called "The Electro/Portable". Interesting to note in the colors below, that the No. 21 Electro/Portable Lamp Base was still made in 1926. Colors: crystal-frosted (shown), plain crystal, and a rare find in moongleam. The moongleam would be from No. 21 Electro/Portable Lamp Base (9″ high) produced in 1926. Records indicate that ½ turn was the produced amount. This relates to about 100 pieces. Current value, $35.00 - 45.00.

14. No. 5, (6″) with No. 1519 Epergnette.
Shown only to present a Heisey Epergnette. Current value, $15.00 - 18.00.

Heisey

GOOD HOUSEKEEPING,
SEPT., 1938

1,2,3,4,5. No. 2, Colonial, circa 1902-1957
Item 1 & 5. 7″ high. Current value, $45.00 - 55.00.
Item 2 & 4. 9″ high. Current value, $65.00 - 75.00.
Item 3. 11″ high. Current value, $90.00 - 120.00.

Rather than show one of each of this pattern, we felt that a full display would be appropriate as it had the longest production life of any Heisey candlestick. Although first issued in 1902 as No. 2-300 Peerless Line, it has continued to present, with the reissue by Imperial (Imperial No. 341); a span of 80 years. The basic pattern of this candlestick was used as a "stepping-stone" to many other items. The No. 300 Candelabras are a good example; there were 8 candelabras along with this basic design. To live the life it has, we feel this had to be the most popular candlestick Heisey produced. Now that it has been added to the "Old Williamsburg" line by Imperial, it may become the most popular there. This item was also made by Heisey as "full-cut"; molded, then all surfaces ground and/or cut for sale as crystal. Colors: crystal (shown); there is a factory record that indicated that No. 2 7″ was produced in moongleam (emerald); the "turn-books" show that in September 1925, one turn made this item in emerald; later in the early part of 1926, one turn produced No. 2 in green; if found in either of these colors, it should be considered very rare. 1958 to present, crystal by Imperial. 1969-1970 Imperial reissued the following colors: blue haze, nut brown, verde, rube, antique blue and amber.

6. No. 1485, Saturn-2 Light, circa 1950, 2½″ high.
Named for the Rings of Saturn. One unique thing about this item is that the large flat top is ground in addition to the bottom surface. This candlestick is a very difficult item to find. Colors: limelight shown. We know of no other colors. Current value, $200.00 - 230.00.

7. No. 1503, circa 1937-1957, 2″ high.
Also known as No. 1503 hurricane block when used with either a 9″ or 11″ hurricane shade. Reissued by Imperial (1957-1975) in crystal. Colors: crystal shown. No other colors known. Current value, $18.00 - 20.00

Heisey

8. No. 1503, circa 1937-1957, Square, 1½″ high.
Reissued by Imperial (1957-1975) in crystal. Colors: crystal shown. No other colors known. Current value, $10.00 - 15.00.
Other Heisey candlesticks having been issued as No. 1503 are as follows:

No. 1503 - 1 lite, 4″ high.

No. 1503 - Candleblock, 2″ high (same type as item 8 except it is round). Reissued by Imperial (1957-1976) in crystal as No. 1503/80. Also (1969-1970) in ruby.

No. 1503 - 2 lite with bobeches & "D" prisms.

No. 1503 - 3 lite shown on plate 23.

9. No. 1540, Lariat Dish, circa 1940-1957, 2″ high.
There are three other lariat candlesticks that we are aware of. Our problem is the item numbers. A 2-lite was issued with the same number. If it has a prefix or dish number, we are not aware of it. In 1942, a Blackout Lamp was issued which consisted of a low-handled dish-type candleholder with a hurricane shade. The third candlestick is a "Small Blackout Lamp". For information on this item, see Plate 24, item 5. Colors: made only in crystal. Current value, $10.00 - 15.00.

10,11,12. No. 1632, Console Set "Lodestar", circa 1956.
Consists of: 2 No. 1632 Candle Centerpieces (candlesticks) and 1 No. 1632 Deep Fruit, floral or salad bowl. Do not confuse this set with "Satellite". Satellite is the same basic pattern (1632), but the star is frosted which makes it "appear to be carved from solid glass" (statement from Heisey advertisement). Colors: dawn (shown), crystal. Current value, items 10 & 12, $45.00 - 50.00. Current value item 11, $70.00 - 80.00.

13. No. 121, Swirl, circa 1929, 2″ high.
Another version of this candlestick is No. 122. The only difference is the swirls on top of the curved surface. The swirls reverse themselves about mid-point of the socket. Colors: flamingo (shown), possibly can be found in moongleam. Current value, $18.00 - 20.00.

Heisey

1

2

3

4

5

6

7

8

9

10

11

12

13

Heisey

Heisey ad from Ladies Home Journal, May, 1940

1,2,3. No. 135, Console Set, circa 1929-1937.
Consists of: 2 No. 135 Candlesticks, 6″ high and 1 No. 135 Bowl. This candlestick was also used for the following patterns: No. 9010 Pan, No. 456 Titania, and No. 458 Olympiad. Colors: sahara (shown), crystal, moongleam, flamingo, alexanderite, and stiegal blue. Current value, $70.00 - 85.00.

4. No. 1, circa 1900-1930, 9″ high.
Originally issued as 1-300 "Peerless Line". It was also 11″ high. This candlestick has been identified by Heisey Collectors of America (see front reference on glass societies) as being Heisey's first candlestick. It was introduced in the year 1900. A 1910 sales catalog also indicates that it was cut on all surfaces. This item with a cut surface sold for $30.00 (regular price was $3.60). This is almost 8 times the regular price. In 1910, even $3.60 was an expensive item. The 11″ candlestick with surface cut sold for much more. Current value, $40.00 - 45.00.

5. No. 68, Hepplewhite, circa 1915-1924, 9″ high.
Etched pattern unknown to us. It should be noted that this is a difficult candlestick to find. We have never seen another for sale. It is mold-marked with the ⟨H⟩ on the socket. Colors: only made in crystal. Current value, $40.00 - 45.00.

6. No. 100, circa 1923-1930, 9″ high.
Design patent No. 68966. Issued March 17, 1923, designed by A. H. Heisey himself. Mold-marked with the ⟨H⟩ on the socket. Colors: crystal-socket and base plain, column has "sponge" finish (frosted). We know of no other colors. Current value, $38.00 - 42.00.

7. No. 4, circa 1902-1917, 9″ high.
Originally issued as No. 4-300 "Peerless Line". This candlestick was also offered as "full cut". (see item 4 above). Unlike a number of the so-called Colonial candlesticks (early numbered) this one was made only in the 9″ size. Colors: crystal only. Current value, $40.00 - 45.00.

8. No. 63-1567, Plantation - 1 light, circa 1957, 4″ high.
Other candlesticks in the pattern:
No. 64-1567 candle block
No. 65-1567 footed epergne candleholder (footed bowl with candle-socket)
No. 66-1567 2-lite candlestick
No. 67-1567 3-lite candelabra. Consists of: 2 No. 1503 bobeche 10 "A" prisms
No. 1567 3-light candlestick

Colors: crystal shown. We are not aware of any other colors. Current value, $60.00 - 65.00.

Heisey

1

2

3

4

5

6

7

8

9

10

11

12

Heisey

9,10,11. No. 4044, New Era, circa 1935-1938, 9″ high.

Item 9. Take a close look at this candlestick. The base is notched on the edge. The center of the "U" (two legs) is different. The sockets are ribbed to receive a different shape bobeche. The base has the same step rise. Now, is it Heisey? As of this writing, we do not think so. We felt that it was important to show it for comparison as the shape, if not Heisey, could be misrepresented. Current value, $20.00 - 30.00.

Item 10. No. 4044 2-lite with No. 4044 bobeches and 20 "A" prisms. Current value, $35.00 - 40.00.

Item 11. No. 4044 Plain. Made in crystal only. Current value, $25.00 - 35.00.

12. No. 112, circa 1926-1957, 3″ high.
Design Patent No. 70558, designed by T. Clarence Heisey, patent date: March 26, 1926, reissued by Imperial in 1976 in crystal. A tall version (9″ high) was produced in the same basic pattern and was listed as No. 123. This candlestick was used for a number of etchings and cuttings in its life span. Some are as follows:

Etchings: Antarctic, Minuet, Olympiad, Orchid, Rose, Springtime and Titania.

Cuttings: Barcelona, Boquet, Continental, Evelyn, Festoon, Wreath, Harvester, Jungle Flower, Piccadilly and Larkspur.

Colors: hawthorn (shown), crystal, moongleam, flamingo, and sahara. Current value, $40.00 - 45.00.

Heisey

A 1938 Good Housekeeping Advertisement. Notice that there are no prisms on this No. 300-three light candelabrum. It is not a Heisey advertisement. It was an ad for Community Plate Silver. Interesting that a silver plate company would use just glass in their advertisement. Not only is it different, but it is also a Christmas advertisement which read; "Next to Tulle and Lohengrin a bride-to-be's main thought is silver". Interesting to say the least!!

Heisey

#32 CANDLE

1&3. No. 18, 1-lite Candelabrum, circa 1910-1920.
Consists of:
     1 No. 18/1 base
     6 6½″ "C" prisms
     6 5″ "C" prisms
     1 No. 7 bobeche
     1 No. 5 candleholder (socket)
     1 No. 54 ferrule

Was also available with "A" or "B" prisms. This item was also made without prisms and carried the same number. Various sizes were as follows: No. 17, 16″ high (with and without prisms) and No. 19, 22″ high (with and without prisms). Interesting to note that No. 17 was shown in a 1929-1930 catalog and the others were not. The larger sizes must not have done as well. Made only in crystal. Current value, $125.00 - 150.00.

2. No. 7039, Gothic, circa 1930, 12″ high.
Also listed as No. 402, 2-Light Base. The socket was made to include 2 No. 402 bobeches with either "A" prisms or "C" prisms. Colors: crystal (shown), sahara, steigle blue, and steigle base, with crystal top. Current values $75.00 - 100.00.

4. No. 150, Saucer Foot, circa 1907, 2″ high.
Also known as Banded Flute. Was used with No. 2 & 3 bedroom sets. We know of no other color than crystal. Current value, $35.00 - 40.00.

5. No. 23, circa 1910-1920, 9″ high.
Few early candlesticks by Heisey can be found with engraved cuttings. This "open rose" cutting is the only one we have ever seen on a No. 33 Pattern. This item was also produced in 3½″ (toy) 5″, 7″, and 11″ high. Made only in crystal. The No. 33 3½″ toy was reissued by Imperial in 1981 as No. 13794 3½″ miniature. Current value, $40.00 - 45.00 plain.

6,7,8. No. 32, Handled, circa 1910-1920

Item 6 No. 32, 7″ high. Current value, $45.00 - 50.00.

Item 7 No. 32, 5″ high. Current value, $30.00 - 35.00.

Item 8 No. 13801, 5″ high, reissued by Imperial in 1981. (reissued in crystal). Current value, $10.00 - 15.00. No. 32 handled was used for 2 bedroom sets in 1931, No. 352 bedroom set and colonial bedroom set. We are not aware of any color except crystal.

9,10,11. No. 1433, Thumbprint and Panel Console Set, circa 1935.
Consists of: 2 No. 1433 Candlesticks and 1 No. 1433 Bowl. We are not totally sure of the length of time these items were produced, as only one listing in 1935 has been found to date, therefore, it helps explain the difficulty in finding various colors in this pattern. No etchings or cuttings are known for this item. Colors: moongleam (shown), crystal, crystal with mirrow finish, flamingo, sahara, and blue (cobalt). Current value, $50.00 - 75.00.

Heisey

1

2

3

4

5

6

7

8

9

10

11

OVAL SHAPE

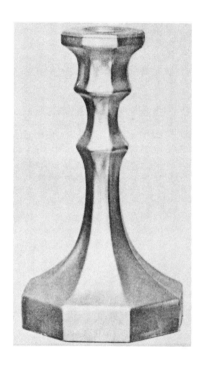

1&3. Leaf and Vine, circa 1923, 10¾" high.
Lustre Candlestick - opaque white with leaf and vine decoration on a clear glass body with applied cobalt blue socket and base. Current value, $75.00-100.00.

2. Drag Loop, circa 1923, 10¾" high.
Lustre Candlestick - opaque white with green drag loop decoration on a clear glass body with applied cobalt blue socket and base. Current value, $80.00 - 110.00. These three candlesticks were produced in the fall of 1923 under the very close supervision of Emil Larson and/or Oscar Eckstead. These two men were hired from Durand just previous to this date to bring an "Art" glass to Imperial. Imperial "free hand" glass is becoming very difficult to find and is reaching a well-deserved status with collectors of art glass.

4. No. 320, Rubigold, circa 1920-1930, 8¼" high.
Can also be found with a twisted optic base and in a No. 320/1 low (shown in cut). No. 320/1 and No. 320/2 (tall) were used for No. 451 Ringing Rock Crystal - Monticello pattern. Colors: rubigold (shown), amber, green and rose marie. Used with various console sets. Current value, $45.00 - 55.00.

5. No. 41, circa 1910-1929, 7" high.
Colors: crystal (shown), amber, mulberry, peacock, and nuruby. Current value, $14.00 - 16.00.

6. Imperial Shelf Sign, circa 1960-1970.
Coloring was added to assist in photographing the details. The stemware is still difficult to see in the middle of the sign. No value placed.

7&8. No. 419, circa 1910-1929, 9" high.
Colors: nuruby and mulberry (shown), crystal, amber, and peacock. Current value, $22.00 - 26.00.

9. No. 1950/81, 5" Handled, circa 1950-1960, 1" high.
Another listing in 1966 shows the same candlestick in milk glass but it has a round footed base which makes the candlestick about 3" high. The footed/handled candlestick carries the same issue number (1950/81). Current value, $8.00 - 12.00.

Imperial

1

2

3

4

5

6

7

8

9

10

11

12

13

10. No. 51785JA, Shen, circa 1935-1981, 2¼″ high.
    1935 The basic mold used for this candlestick was No. 699 - Washington. The mold was converted in 1946 to No. 5020/3 Cathay. Colors were verde and cranberry. The 1981 reissue is imperial jade. Current value, $30.00 - 32.00.

11. No. 6007, circa 1910-1929, 7″ high.
    This pattern can also be found 9″ high and is No. 6009. In the 1920's, No. 6007 was issued with a console set using No. 5141/2B, 8½″ salad bowl (three footed) and was known as special lot 2074. Colors: sapphire iridescent (shown), nuruby iridescent, and peacock iridescent. Current value, $18.00 - 22.00.

12. No. 7802C, Crocheted, 2½″ high.
    This candleholder was made as a candle-lamp (shade missing) for the exclusive sales to Sears Roebuck. The special label shown was attached to each piece. Only made in crystal. Current value, $16.00 - 20.00.

13. No. 414/1, Diamond Quilted, circa 1920-1930, 2½″ high.
    (Named by Hazel Marie Weatherman) Colors: green (shown), rose pink, and light blue. There is a possibility that it may be found in amber and a very rare find in black. Current value, $12.00 - 14.00.

Imperial

A NEW GIFT ITEM
IN THE **CANDLEWICK** LINE!

*Imperial's
Flower Candle
Holder*

A graceful miniature
epergne! Used singly on a
small table for two . . . a
pair or set of four on large
table and buffet!

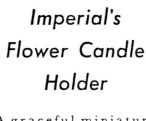

**Hand-crafted,
perfect,
clear crystal,
Retails $1.00 each**

Garden enthusiasts will take to this item quickly because
it provides an ingenious way to utilize flowers and candles
for small table decoration.

For detailed information write to

IMPERIAL GLASS CORPORATION
Bellaire, Ohio

*Makers of patent-protected hand-crafted Cape Cod,
Twist, Etiquette, Continental and other patterns.*

Imperial

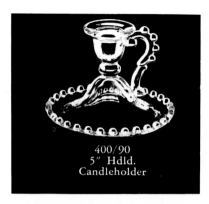

400/90
5" Hdld.
Candleholder

400/90
5 inch Handled Candleholder

400/80
3½ inch Low Candleholder

400 79
2-Pce. Hurricane Lamp

1&3. No. 400/90, Handled, circa 1947-1967, 5" high.
The first issue of this candlestick was made with a deep cupped base and later issues (we believe about 1960 on) has the shallow cupped base. The shallow cupped base is shown. Current value, $18.00 - 20.00.

2. No. 400/115, 3-Way, circa 1941, 3" high.
Also issued as No. 400/15 31B as part of a 3 piece console set. Current value, $28.00 - 32.00.

4&5. No. 1950/170, Low Leaf Pattern, circa 1950-1971, 1½" high.
These items were made in 1978 for the Imperial Glass Collectors Society and are so mold marked. Item 4 is very rare as it was an experimental color and 24 were produced. Item 5 had a production of about 300. This color will not be reissued as agreed by Imperial Glass Collectors Society. Current value, item 4, $70.00 - 80.00. Current value item 5, $35.00 - 40.00.

6. No. 400/80, circa 1939-1976, 3½ high.
Other uses were as follows:
No. 400/80/2 Eagle Candleholder
No. 400/8013B 3 Piece Consolet Set
No. 400/8063B 3 Piece Console Set
No. 400/8075B 3 Piece Console Set
Current value, $8.00 - 10.00.

7. No. 400/81, Handled, circa 1937-1943, 3½" high.
Same as item 6 with the exception of the added handle. Other uses were: No. 400/63B/81 3 Piece Console Set and No. 400/81/2 Eagle Candleholder (Patent No. 13431210-1942) and No. 400/76 Hurricane Lamp. Current value, $10.00 - 14.00.

8. Paden City No. 444.
Shown for comparison with item 10. The glass is a little heavier and quality is not quite as good. Cu rrent value, $24.00 - 28.00.

9. No. 400/152R, 3 Piece Hurricane Lamp, circa 1943-1952, 14" high.
Consists of:
No. 400/79R Candleholder (reissued in 1974 as No. 14780)
No. 400/152 Chimney-plain top rim
No. 400/152 Adapter
Can be found as No. 400/152 and the only difference is the chimney which has a crimpled (crimped) top rim. Current value, $30.00 - 36.00.

10. No. 400/100, Twin, circa 1939-1968.
Other uses were:
No. 400/127L 4 Piece Console Set
No. 400/920F 3 Piece Console Set
No. 400/1006B 3 Piece Console Set
No. 400/6300B 3 Piece Console Set
Current value, $24.00 - 28.00.

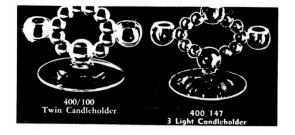

400/100
Twin Candleholder

400 147
3 Light Candleholder

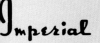

1

2

3

4

5

6

7

8

9

10

Imperial

1&5. No. 700, Panel, circa 1910-1929, 7″ - 7½″ high.
Reissued in 1950 in crystal with the "Eagle" Candleholder and was listed as No. 700/777/2, 7″ "Eagle" Candleholder. Colors: plain amber (shown), nugreen, mulberry, and crystal. Current value, $18.00 - 22.00.

2,3,4. Special Lot 2089 Peacock, circa 1910-1929.
Consists of:

    2 No. 635 candlesticks 8½″ high
    1 No. 6569/2B 12″ bowl

This console set was issued in a number of ways. Listed below are a few:

    3 Piece Console Sets (shown)
    Special Lot 2088 Nuruby
    Special Lot 2090 Sapphire
    4 Piece Console Sets. Same as shown with a 14″ plate for the No. 6569/2B bowl
    Special Lot 2082 Nuruby
    Special Lot 2083 Peacock
    Special Lot 2084 Sapphire

Special lot 2018 (same as shown with a No. 634 black base for bowl). Colors: nuruby iridescent, peacock iridescent, and plain mulberry. For additional candlestick information see items 12, 13, and 14 below. Current value, $22.00 - 28.00.

6. No. 51218, Linear Stacking, circa 1980-1981, 4¼″ high.
This candlestick is made to allow a number to be stacked. It is also a reversible candlestick. As shown, it is used with a large candle. Turned over, it has a socket for a standard candle. Made only in crystal. Current value, $8.00 - 10.00.

7. No. 71790, Smithsonian, circa 1976-1981, 5½″ high.
This article was first made under a license to create an exact reproduction from an early piece of glass owned by the Smithsonian Institution. It is identified (mold-Si) as a Smithsonian reproduction. Colors: crystal shown. Also made in sapphire (blue). Current value, $14.00 - 18.00.

1   2   3   4   5

6   7   8   9   10

11   12   13   14.

8. Twisted Optic, circa 1920-1930, 4″ high.
Amber shown. Other known colors are green and rose marie.
Current value, $12.00 - 14.00.

9. Three Face-Colonial.
This candlestick is shown to illustrate the type of items made for the Smithsonian Institution. The Smithsonian will release this item for sale in 1982. It was loaned to us by Imperial for publication in this book. No value placed.

10. No. 51789, Glacier, circa new 1979, 3½″ high.
We are not aware that it was made in any color other than crystal.
Current value, $8.00 - 10.00.

11. Northwood, circa 1915, 9″ high.
Shown for comparison. This candlestick appears, at first glance, to be Imperial No. 635 but, sitting side by side, one can see the distinct difference between them. Colors: green satin shown.
Current value, $35.00 - 40.00.

12,13,14. No. 635, circa 1910-1929, 8½″ high.
These three items are shown to extend the coverage from the console set shown (items 2, 3 & 4). Item 12 has a silver deposit design on the base, knobs, and top of socket. We have found very little of the early Imperial glass with silver deposit (overlay). Item 13 is shown for its color, a color between vaseline and canary. We can find no listing for this color for the years this item was made. Item 14 is No. 635/3 Twisted Optic. The only difference between this and the other is the twisted base design. These candlesticks were listed as available in the following colors: crystal, amber, mulberry, peacock and nuruby. Current value, $22.00 - 32.00.

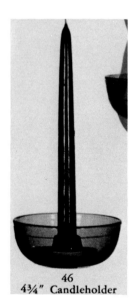

46
4¾″ Candleholder

HOFFMAN HOUSE

1886/285
Square
Candleholder

STAMM HOUSE
DEWDROP OPALESCENT

1886/2850
2 Pc.
Hurricane
Lamp

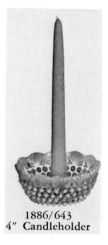

1886/643
4″ Candleholder

Imperial candlesticks from a company brochure.

Imperial

1&3. No. 1950/80 "Vinelf", circa 1950-1965, 7½" high.
The two shown are of a late vintage. The mold has been reworked (ring around base). The early candlesticks do not have this ring. Colors: white doe skin (milk glass) and verde (shown), light blue, and gold on black. Current value, $28.00 - 34.00.

2. No. 41696, Collectors Crystal Hurricane Lamp, circa 1980-1981. Colors: horizon blue (shown), crystal. Current value, $18.00 - 22.00.

4&8. No. 727R, "Molly", circa 1935-1940, 2" high. (Named by Hazel Marie Weatherman)
Some doubt exists with these candlesticks. McKee made a similar item No. 156 Optic Octagon Edge. We did not find the McKee listing until after the ones shown were photographed. Until proved otherwise, we will list these as Imperial. Colors: amber (shown) with frosted edges. Can also be found in rose pink, green and crystal. Current value, $18.00 - 20.00.

5. No. 637, "Intaglio", circa 1930-1935, 3½" high.
This must have been a very limited production item. We have yet to find another of its kind. Colors: crystal with painted intaglio grapes in white, pink background-fired. Current value, $22.00 - 26.00.

6. No. 1590, Zodiac, circa 1969-1970, 5⅝" high.
This item was made from a reworked Heisey mold. It now bears an "IG" mold mark. It should still be considered a Heisey reissue. Zodiac figures on this item are as follows: Jupiter Pluvius in the center, Capricorn and Sagittarius on one socket: Taurus and Leo on the other socket. Colors: verde (shown), crystal, and amberglo. Current value, $38.00 - 42.00

41790 7-3/8" Tall
Candleholder

7. No. 637, Gold Encrusted.
Decorated with a gold deposit. This decoration appears to be a typical "Lotus" type (not believed to be by Imperial). Can also be found with a diamond quilted base. Colors: amber, green, rose marie and crystal. Current value, $30.00 - 34.00.

9. No. 4190, "Short", circa 1980, 5½" high.
This item was issued in 1980 as part of the "Collectors Crystal" Group. Made only in crystal. Current value, $10.00 - 12.00.

10&11. No. 4179, "Tall", circa 1920-1981, 7⅜" high.
This candlestick has had one of the longer lives at Imperial. We have found them painted, dipped in paint, sprayed with paint; anything to color it. The only color we are aware of is carmel slag (shown) and made in 1973-74. It was also made in purple slag that year. We have not seen one, but there is a possibility that one can be found in End-O'day-Ruby, another slag color made the same year. In 1974-75, this item was issued with "Fired Gold on Crystal", 22 kt. gold fired into the glass after being hand decorated. These should be the desired collectable. Current value, $28.00 - 36.00.

12. No. 780, Star-Holly, circa 1950-1955, 3" high.
First introduced in milk glass (decorated) and did not market well. About 1951 was made in plain milk glass. Colors: no other color known. Amber believed to be experimental (not a production item). Current value, $40.00 - 50.00.

FINE ROCK CRYSTAL CONSOLE SETS
Six sets to carton, shipping weight 50 pounds

734W/cut 451. 3-piece, per set, $5.00

No. 451   Ringing Rock Crystal Monticello Pattern

Imperial

1&3. No. 5107 Wedding Lamp, Circa 1949-1952, 12" high.
Part of Cathay Glass Line which included two other colors: cranberry and verde surface treated (satin finish). Current value, $40.00 - 45.00.

2. No. 11/119 Crucifix, Circa 1906-1950, 9½" high.
In 1906 this item was also made in "Purple Colored Glass" and listed as No. 30/119. Reissued in crystal as No. 119 and in milk glass as No. 1950/119. Current value, $35.00 - 40.00.

4. No. 0252 Smoke Shade, Circa 1904-1910, 6" high.
Also known as "Smoke Bell". This item was for hanging over a candlestick or oil lamp to break up the smoke and to keep the smoke from making a ring on the ceiling. No. 252 is same shade but in crystal. Current Value, $18.00 - 20.00.

5. No. 1950-137 Double Grape, Circa 1950, 3½" high.
This is one of the first items to carry the ⊄ moldmark. No other color known. Current Value, $24.00 - 26.00.

6,7,8. No. 1950-325 (candlestick only), Circa 1960-1973, 3¼" high.
Console set shown in Doe-skin finish with oil lamp flower vase. The Doe-skin finish was an Imperial-Lenox issue. Current value, $14.00 - 22.00.

9. No. 1950-330, Circa 1960-1966, 7½" high.
Other known colors are verde and azelea. Current value, $20.00 - 24.00.

330
7½" Tall
Candleholder

203F
7½" Footed Bowl

No. 451 Ringing Rock Crystal Monticello Pattern

From an Imperial catalog.

Imperial

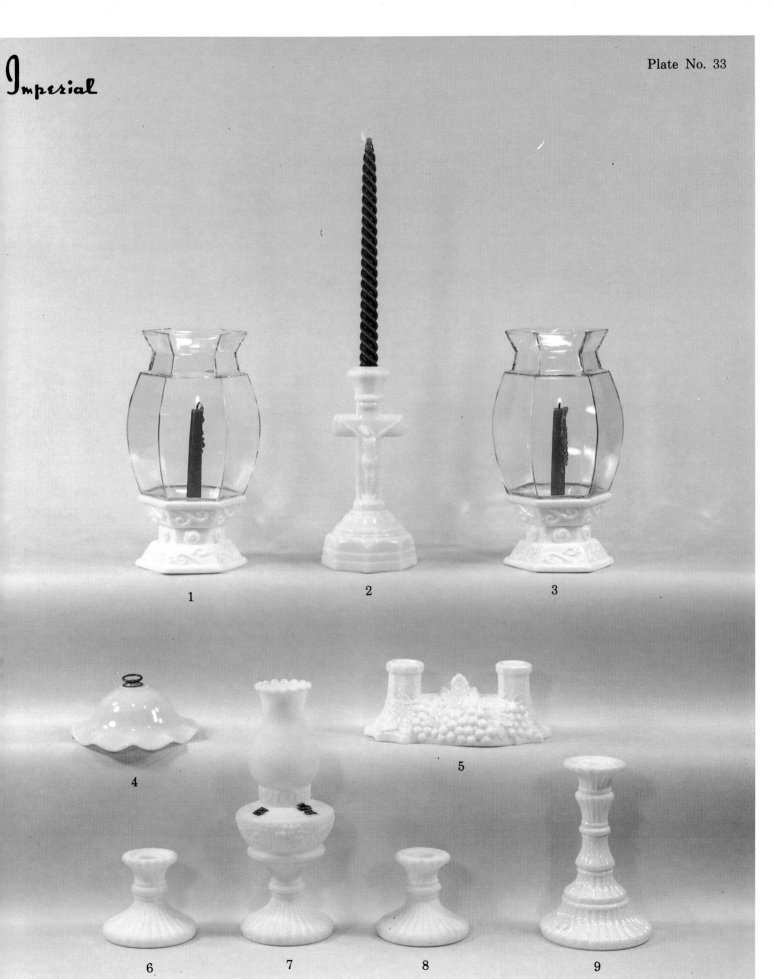

1   2   3

4   5

6   7   8   9

Imperial

607—10″ Oval Candle Bowl

1. No. 2920 Collectors Crystal, circa 1957-1980.
   1980 reissue was in color as shown. Very few colors were issued in the Collectors Crystal. Candlesticks in this pattern are difficult to find other than the one shown. In 1957 No. 292 (Candle Bowl) was issued with or without a shade (No. 1920 being with shade). This reissue changed the shade from a standard lamp (Hurricane type) to the more modern shown. The shade shown was adapted from the No. 51950 Hurricane Lamp. Current value, $24.00 - 28.00.

2. No. 607 Oval Candle Bowl, circa 1950-1979.
   The first records that we have list the item in milk glass as No. 1950-607. The first record we have showing it in crystal is in 1957. We are not aware of any other colors. Current value, $35.00 - 45.00.

3. No. 51513F Fantasy Frost, circa 1979-1980, 9″ high.
   No other colors known. Current value, $8.00 - 10.00.

4&8. No. 42786, circa 1950-1975, 3″ high.
   This item is mold marked with the ℂ as shown in the pattern detail and a view of the bottom. This is a reissue in 1974-75 when it was produced in "White Carnival". The item could be from the 1966 carnival issues in the purple iridescent. Also known as amethyst. "Carnival" is a trade name used by Imperial for iridescent glass. Current value, $38.00 - 44.00.

5,6,7. No. 42788, circa 1980-1981, 3″ high.
   These three items are shown together to demonstrate the various treatments that the finishers might put on any given piece of glass. This creates problems as some collectors may not accept the items as indicated when these variants differ so much: item 5 — flat base, item 6 — bell shaped base, and item 7 — rolled rim, semi-bell base. Colors: pink carnival (shown), meadow green carnival, and amethyst carnival. Current value, $6.00 - 8.00.

9&13. Threaded Socket. Item 9. "Threaded Socket" with roses on base, circa 1950-1981, 3½″ high.
   No. 51784S shown crystal satin 1980-1981. Patterns:
   - No. 1950-160 milk glass early 1950's-1966
   - No. 42784 amber carnival 1974-1975
   - No. 42784 white carnival 1974-1975
   - No. 42784 pink carnival 1978 only
   - No. 42784HB horizon blue carnival 1980-1981
   - No. 43784 purple slag 1974-1975
   - No. 43784 end o'day ruby 1974-1976
   - No. 43784 jade slag 1974-1976
   - No. 43784 caramel slag 1975-1976
   - No. 51791PKS pink satin 1980-1981.

   Current value, $6.00 - 8.00.

   Item 13. "Threaded Socket" with grapes on base, circa 1950-1981.
   No. 51784BLS shown. Blue Satin 1979-1981. Patterns:
   - No. 1950/880 milk glass early 1950's-1966
   - No. 42782 amber carnival 1974-1975
   - No. 51784 ivory satin 1978-1981.

   Change of pattern numbers. See items below. Pattern can be found in basic shape with "Stipple-Marble" design No. 675. Current value, $6.00 - 8.00.

10,11,12. Console Set, circa 1980-1981.
   Consists of: No. 42788AT Candlesticks (2) and No. 42702AT 9″ Crimped Bowl. Shown only for its amethyst carnival glass. For candlesticks details, see items 5,6,7 above. Current value, $6.00 - 10.00.

Imperial

1

2

3

4

5

6

7

8

9

10

11

12

13

Re-issues

301
2-Lite Candelabra

301
3-Lite Candelabra

1513
3-Lite Candelabra Epergne

300/0
1-Lite
Candelabra

4044
2-Lite
Candelabra

1509
1-Lite
Candelabra

142/147
3-Lite
Candleholder

134/100
2-Lite
Candleholder
"Waverly"

1540
2-Lite
Candleholder

1506
1-Lite
Candleblock

1503/80
1-Lite
Candleblock

Imperial Glass Corporation, Bellaire, Ohio

Imperial

#32 CANDLE

1&4. No. 51224 Hurricane Lamp, circa 1979-1981, 9¾" high.
Colors: amber and ebony shown. Other known color is crystal.
Current value, $12.00 - 14.00.

2. No. 16990 Hurricane Lamp, circa 1950-1981, 11½" high.
First issued as Cape Cod No. 160/79, Hurricane Lamp, 9" high,
(smaller shade), in the early 1950's. Made only in crystal. Current
value, $18.00 - 22.00.

3. No. 51522(PKS) Hurricane Lamp, circa 1980-1981, 11¾" high.
Colors: pink satin shown. Other known colors are blue satin and
satin crystal. Current value, $16.00 - 18.00.

5,6,7. Heisey Reissue by Imperial

Item 5 No. 13795 Miniature Chamber-stick,
circa 1981, 1½" high
(Heisey No. 31 toy). Current value, $8.00 - 10.00.

Item 6 No. 13794 Miniature, circa 1981, 3½" High.
(Heisey No. 33) Do not confuse with
Imperial No. 700. See Plate 30.
Current value, $10.00 - 15.00

Item 7 No. 13801 Chamber-stick, circa 1980-1981, 5" high.
(Heisey No. 32). Current value, $12.00 - 18.00.

5,6,7, made only in crystal.

8. No. 753 3-Light, circa 1934-1951, 7" high.
Known as Viking Rock Crystal when used for cut design on base.
This is the first of its kind (3-light) ever manufactured by
Imperial. Made only in crystal. In 1943 to 1950 was used for the
following:
No. 753/777/1-2   3-Piece Eagle Candleholder
No. 753/777/   2-Piece Eagle Candleholder
No. 753/777/H.L   5-Piece Hurricane Lamp
Other use for console sets:
No. 0/378/75 Satin Sunburst
No. 75BX/42 Satin Scroll
No. 75/CUT 261 (cut pattern on set)
No. 754/CUT 261 (cut pattern on set)
No. 75BX/CUT 280 (cut pattern on set)
No. 734/75/CUT 280 (cut pattern on set)
No. 754/CUT 465 (cut pattern on set)
No. 320/75CUT 465 (cut pattern on set)
No. 734A/75/CUT 465 (cut pattern on set)
Current value, $30.00 - 34.00.

9. No. 753 2-Light, circa 1934-1951, 6" high.
As can be seen on base (color for photographing only), cutting
No. 280 is used. Although we do not have a listing of the console
sets as with 3-light, we believe the general use was about the same.
Current value, $28.00 - 32.00.

We are not aware of any colors in Item 8 and 9.

10,11,14,15. No. 153 Twin (Rope), circa 1925-1935, 4½" high.
Also known as Newbound. In the early 1950's was issued in milk
glass as No. 1950/100. All colors were made before 1950. Colors:
ritz blue, milk glass, amber and stiegel green (shown), crystal, rose
pink and imperial green. Console set usage as follows: No. 1535
3 Piece Oval, No. 153 3 Piece Round. Current value, $15.00 - 20.00.

Imperial

12&13. No. 671, circa 1925-1935, 7″ high.
These items carry the same issue number, but the base is different. Item 13 was named "Amelia" by Hazel Marie Weatherman, therefore, we refer to it as that. We are not aware of any colors in these two patterns. Current value, $10.00 - 14.00.

HIGH GRADE HAND CUTTINGS ON EXTRA POLISHED CRYSTAL

SPECIAL LOT 2064 contains 9 pairs of Hand Cut Candlesticks, (all different) and 1 dozen assorted 2 piece Hand Cut Night Sets.

The 9 pairs of Candlesticks consist of ⅙ dozen each of 3 sizes shown, each in 3 cuttings shown.

6247 Cut 61. Square. 7 inch High.

6249 Cut 63. Square. 9 inch High.

62412 Cut 66. Square. 12 inch High.

Imperial

1   2   3   4

5   6   7   8   9

10   11   12   13   14   15

*51792 9"
Dolphin
Candleholder

1,4,5,6,7,8. No. 779 Empire Pattern, circa 1914-1981, 5″ high.
All shown because of periods released.

1 & 4. Hurricane Lamps, circa 1920-1925. Shades are frosted with fruit designs. Current value, $35.00 - 38.00.

5. Blue No. 4/779, circa 1920-1930. Current value, $12.00 - 14.00.

6 & 7. Ebony with gold decoration, circa 1951-1955. Also made in plain black satin this same period. Current value, $16.00 - 20.00.

8. Crystal, circa 1920-1930. Produced in 1950 in milk glass No. 1950-779. Produced in 1966-67 in caramel slag. Reissued in 1981 in pink carnival No. 42793PK. Can be found in amber (1920-1930) and green (green is a rare color). Current value, $10.00 - 12.00.

2&3. No. K-15 Sandwich Dolphin, circa 1974-1981, 9½″ high.
These candlesticks were originally made for the Metropolitan Museum of Art and were sold only at the museum and the Boston and Sandwich Museum in Sandwich, Mass. They are mold marked on the base "MMA". It was first believed that the reproductions were reissued (made from the old molds) but further investigation found that they were made from new molds. It should be noted that the original molds are in possession of the Metropolitan Museum of Art. The Blue Dolphin was a gift from Imperial in 1979. Colors: sky blue and emerald shown. Also made in Crystal. Current value, $40.00 - 45.00.

9,10,11. No. 1950/90, circa 1950-1981, 9″ high.
This item had an early issue, but for a number of years (believed to be between 1955 and 1973) was not made. In 1974 it was reissued in crystal as No. 51782. In 1976 it was made in new colors — nut brown, ultra blue (shown — Item 9) and fern green. In 1980 it was issued as No. 42792HB in horizon blue carnival. The three shown appear to be different; they are not. Although made from different molds (Item 9 & 11) only Item 10 is a finished product. Item 9 and 11 still have the "over pour" from the mold which has not been ground off (notice difference in the "over pour"). The milk glass is the oldest, being first made in 1950 as No. 1950/90. Current value, $20.00 - 26.00.

Imperial

1

2

3

4

5

6

7

8

9

10

11

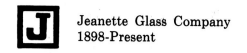

1&3. Cosmos Candle Vases, circa 1950's.
Candlestick 3″ high and candle vases 9″ high. The vase has a candle socket making it a hurricane shade. Colors: Crystal with white decoration. May also be found in golden iridescent with white decoration. Current value, $6.00 - 8.00.

2. Cosmos 3-Light with vase, circa 1940-1950.
Candlestick 5″ high and vases 5″ high. Colors: crystal candlestick; vases with white decoration. Current value, $12.00 - 14.00.

4. 2-Light Vase, circa 1935-1940, 8″ high.
Colors: crystal shown. We are not aware of any other colors. Current value, $18.00 - 22.00.

5. Louisa 2-Light, circa 1950-1960, 5″ high.
Colors: crystal (shown), floragold iridescent, pink, blue, and green. Current value, $10.00 - 12.00.

6. Low, circa 1950's, 3″ high.
This item is shown to allow a better view of the base-candlestick used for Item 1 & 3 above; it is the same candlestick with gold decoration on the base. Current value, $8.00 - 10.00.

7&8. No. 26, circa 1915-1926, 7″ high.

7. Notice slight difference in size, body and height. This is a different mold from Item 8 and we believe it to be a very early mold. The item is "sunturned" indicating that the decoloring agent in the glass was manganese. We believe Item 7 to be made between 1915 and 1918. Current value, $22.00 - 28.00.

8 . Amber shown. Other known color is green. Circa 1926. Current value, $26.00 - 30.00.

9. Iris and Herringbone, circa 1928-1932; 1950; 1970, 5½″ high.
Also known as just "Iris". Colors: iridescent shown. Other known colors are crystal, crystal frosted and amber. There is a possibility that it may be found in pink and light blue as other "Iris" items were made in these colors. Current value, $12.00 - 14.00.

10. No. 1774 Laurel (band on base), circa 1950's, 5″ high.
Was used with No. 1700 3-light Console Set which had a No. 1761 Console Bowl with it. We are not aware of the other colors, if any, used for this candlestick, but it could be that it had the same colors as "Swirl". Current value, $14.00 - 16.00

We would like to point out two other 2-light candlesticks which used the basic pattern as the Iris and Laurel. One is No. 387/P 2-Light which was also 5″ high. It is very ornate and found in "Shell Pink" milk glass. Made in 1958-1959. We have yet to see one. The other is "Swirl". Swirl was made in pink, opaque blue, and dark blue-green. Made in 1937-1938.

11,12,13. No. 31, circa 1924, 6½″ high.
We have shown these three items to allow for comparison.

11. Crystal with flower decoration. The decoration could be by others (not Jeannette). Current value, $9.00 - 13.00.

12. Crystal with silver overlay, oval base. After this item was photographed, we found out that it is not a Jeannette item, it was made by U.S. Glass, Factory "F", which is the old Ripley & Company. It is listed in a 1919 catalog, see the Special Plates in the U.S. Glass Section. Current value, $10.00 - 14.00.

13. Fired-on color. This was a low-budget item which was used to add cheap color to brighten the drab 1920's. Example is that of a console set; 2 candlesticks, one bowl and a bowl stand would retail for $1.00. $1.00 was a lot in 1924 but if you divide the glass up, the candlesticks would amount to about 25¢ each, the bowl 30¢ and the stand 20¢. Colors: fired-on: blue (shown), orange, purple, and green. Can be found in amber and green in clear glass. Current values, $8.00 - 10.00.

McKee Glass Company
1853-1888 McKee and Brothers, Pittsburgh, Pa.
1888-1903 McKee and Brothers, Jeannette, Pa.
1903-1951 McKee Glass Company, Jeannette, Pa.
1951-1961 Thatcher Glass Company, McKee Div., Jeannette, Pa.
1961-Present, Jeannette Glass Corporation, Jeannette, Pa.

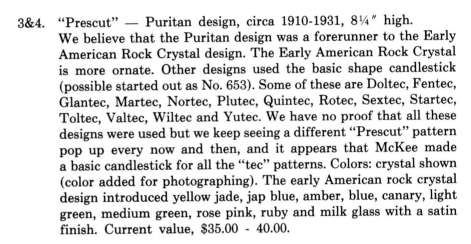

1. Baccarat.
    Shown for comparison with the McKee "Ray". Current value, $75.00 - 100.00.

2&5. "Ray", circa 1910-1930, 8″ high.
    We are not aware of any color except crystal. Current value, $35.00 - 45.00.

3&4. "Prescut" — Puritan design, circa 1910-1931, 8¼″ high.
    We believe that the Puritan design was a forerunner to the Early American Rock Crystal design. The Early American Rock Crystal is more ornate. Other designs used the basic shape candlestick (possible started out as No. 653). Some of these are Doltec, Fentec, Glantec, Martec, Nortec, Plutec, Quintec, Rotec, Sextec, Startec, Toltec, Valtec, Wiltec and Yutec. We have no proof that all these designs were used but we keep seeing a different "Prescut" pattern pop up every now and then, and it appears that McKee made a basic candlestick for all the "tec" patterns. Colors: crystal shown (color added for photographing). The early American rock crystal design introduced yellow jade, jap blue, amber, blue, canary, light green, medium green, rose pink, ruby and milk glass with a satin finish. Current value, $35.00 - 40.00.

6. No. 154 "Carnation" cutting, circa 1920-1930, 8″ high.
    Was advertised as "stone engraved ware" and was sold with No. 154, 9″ Low Foot Console Bowl — Carnation cut. We are not aware of any other colors. Current value, $26.00 - 30.00.

7&11. Laurel, circa 1935-1940, 4″ high.
    This was sometimes referred to as "Laurelware". This basic pattern was also made in "Flower" and "Autumn". Colors: jade green (shown), French ivory, and opal white. The "Flower" pattern can also be found in powder blue. Current value, $18.00 - 22.00.

8. No. 200 Low, circa 1930's, 3½″ high.
    Gold encrusted No. 3 Line, octagon shape. Colors: rose pink shown. We have no other color listing. Current value, $12.00 - 14.00.

9&10. No. 100 5″ Low, circa 1925-1935, 3½″ high.
    (5″ refers to diameter of base.)
    9. Crystal with gold encrusted base. Current value, $10.00 - 12.00.
    10. Crystal with silver overlay-Dogwood pattern. Current value, $18.00 - 22.00.
    Other known uses: Decorated Dresden Lines, Stone Engraved (also known as "Light Cut") "M" pattern, Stone Engraved "V" pattern, Stone Engraved No. 144 pattern. All of the above were available in crystal, amber, green and rose pink.

TRADE MARK

12&16. No. 157 Scallop Edge, circa 1930's, 2″ high.
Also known as R.E. Candlestick. Do not confuse with No. 156 Optic, octagon edge. No. 156 has a heavy rib at each scallop point. Colors: rose pink-gold encrusted shown. Other known color is green. Was also used for etched patterns. One known was "Brocade". If found with plain round edge (known as a "roll" edge), it will be No. 153. Current value, $10.00 - 14.00.

13. Oval Bird of Paradise 2-Light, circa 1930's, 6″ high.
Very difficult to find. Colors: frosted crystal shown. We are not aware of any other colors. Current value, $42.00 - 46.00.

14. Vulcan Design, circa 1915-1925, 6″ high.
Was also used with a boudoir set. Colors: crystal shown. We are not aware of any other colors. Current value, $18.00 - 22.00.

15. 2-Light Early American Rock Crystal, circa 1925-1931, 5″ high.
Can also be found in a 3-light. Colors: crystal shown. See item 3 & 4 above for information on other colors. Current value, $16.00 - 20.00.

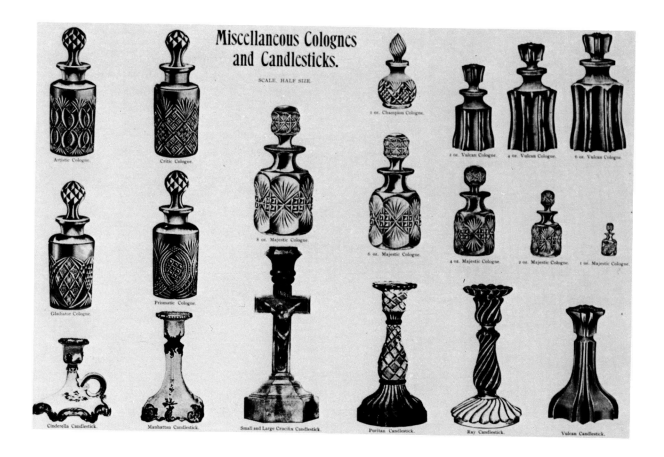

Page from the National Glass Company catalog when McKee & Brothers Glass Works was a part of the National Glass Company Combine. Circa 1894.

1 2 3 4 5 6

7 8 9 10 11

12 13 14 15 16

13-inch Flared Bowl with candle transforms a
centerpiece into a conversation piece

A January 1955 ad in China
Glass & Tablewares for New
Martinsville Glass.

1,2,3,4,5. No. 21-9, circa 1901-1925, 9″ high.
We have shown a variety of this item to point out some of the problems we have had with the research. First, you may wish to see the candlestick shown on Plate 22, Item 1 (Fostoria). Then, look at Plate 42, Item 1 (Paden City). You should read the write-up on both. Items 2, 3 & 4 were bought as a console set. It is true that New Martinsville made a No. 10-21 console set in blue, but here is a case where No. 2394, 12″ Fostoria bowl is used. The shading of the glass is different under close examination. Colors: green, blue and amber (shown), crystal, and amethyst. Amethyst is the most rare. Current value, $22.00 - 30.00.

6&7. No. 14, circa 1901-1937, 5½″ and 7″ high shown.
3½″ and 8½″ high also made. We have shown these items as New Martinsville; We could have just as well shown them as Paden City No. 112. Maybe the only question between the two is Item 6 (5½″ high). We can find no record where Paden City made a 5½″ No. 112 candlestick. They did make a 7″ and 8½″ candlestick. The 5½″ was the driving force for our placement as New Martinsville, Paden City did use No. 112 for engraving and etching, but we have no record of silver deposit (encrusted) as shown. We know of no other colors. Current value, $14.00 - 22.00.

8. No. 11 Colonial, circa 1901-1937, 5½″ high.
No other colors known. Current value, $12.00 - 14.00.

9. No. 4536, circa 1930-1945, 5″ high.
This item was first made by New Martinsville and reissued by Viking. The catalog stated that it could be found in crystal, colors, cuttings frosted and etched. We do not have a list of the colors. Some of the patterns using it are Janice, Wild Rose, Vogue No. 4554/401 and Etched No. 30 pattern. Crystal shown. Current value, $14.00 - 18.00.

10. No. 454, circa 1920-1930, 4″ high.
We know of no other color than crystal. Current value, $14.00 - 16.00.

11&12. No. 12, circa 1901-1920, 7″ high.
Again, we have look-alikes. As we know now, three companies made this type pattern (see Cambridge Plate 7, Item 7 and Paden City No. 113, not shown). The Cambridge No. 73 candlestick does not have as sharp edges as the ones shown and is 6½″ high. New Martinsville made it 3½″, 5½″, 7″ and 8½″ high. These are a toss-up between New Martinsville No. 12 and Paden City No. 113. (Paden City also made the 7″ and 8½″ high.) Colors: crystal and crystal-frosted (shown). We have no listings for any color. Current value, $16.00 - 22.00.

13. No. 4453 Teardrop No. 4400 Line, circa 1940-1950, 6″ high.
First issued by New Martinsville and continued by Viking. Used for etched patterns and silver encrustation as shown. We have no listing of any colors. Current value, $14.00 - 18.00.

14. No. 18 Candelabra, Queen Ann No. 18 Line, circa 1937-1968, 6″ high.
Also used for Radiance No. 4200 Line with bobeches and "U" prisms. An early catalog listed it with shades as No. 18 Hurricane Candlestick. We know it was made in color, but we do not have any records listing them. Current value, $16.00 - 20.00.

From a 1955 New Martinsville ad.

1. No. 169, circa 1901-1937, 7″ high.
   Only made in crystal. Current value, $18.00 - 22.00.

2. No. 16, circa 1901-1937, 8½″ high.
   Used for cutting. One known pattern cut No. 108. Current value, $20.00 - 26.00.

3&7. 3-Light Candelabra, circa 1920-1950, 6½″ high.
   3. No. 5515 Also No. 5516 as an epergne. Current value, $38.00 - 42.00.

   7. No. 425 Also No. 425-2V with ivy vase in center and bobeches and prisms; No. 425-3 with 3 bobeches and prisms.

   Difference between Item 3 and Item 7 is the base. Only made in crystal. Current value, $36.00 - 40.00.

4. No. 17, circa 1901-1937, 8½″ high.
   Used for cutting. One known pattern cut No. 109. Only made in crystal. Current value, $26.00 - 30.00.

5. No. 15, circa 1901-1937, 8½″ high.
   Also made 3½″, 5½″, 7″ high. Made only in crystal. Current value, $28.00 - 32.00.

6. No. 1287 Hurricane Lamp (shade missing), circa 1957, 7″ high.
   The original shade was 10″ high which made the Item 11½″ high. Also known as "Epic" by Viking. Colors: amethyst (shown), smoke-grey, and possibly green. Current value, $12.00 - 16.00.

8. No. 37/2 Moondrops, circa 1933-1940, 4″ high.
   Also made in a 3-Light No. 37/3. Colors: ritz blue (shown), amber rose, evergreen, bury, crystal, and ice blue. Possibly found in light green, jadite, smoke, and black, as this was the complete line of the Moondrops pattern. Current value, $28.00 - 30.00.

9,11,13. Colonial Handled and Plain, circa 1933-1937, 4″ high.
   Colors: amber and white opal (shown), green, and pink. Current value, $6.00 - 10.00.

10. No. 415, circa 1937-1944, 6½″ high.
   We call it "Squirrel" as it appears to be a raised squirrel's tail. This item was also sold as a No. 415 Hurricane Candlestick (without shade). Colors: Made only in crystal. Current value, $16.00 - 20.00.

12. No. 42 2-Light Radiance 4200 Line, circa 1937-1968, 6½″ high.
   Was made and used for various etchings on base. Colors: amber shown. Other known colors are Alice blue and crystal. Current value, $22.00 - 26.00.

14. No. 452 Seal, circa 1937-1944, 7″ high.
   Made only in crystal. Current value, $45.00 - 50.00.

1

2

3

4

5

6

7

8

9

10

11

12

13

14

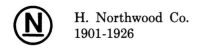
We have tried not to include glass and/or glass house information in this publication unless we had a reliable source for authenticity or direct catalog information. In the case of Northwood glass, we have very little of either. In fact, information is almost as difficult to obtain as Northwood candlesticks. Although the information presented is limited, we felt that the candlesticks shown were important, if for nothing else but to straighten out the Northwood candlesticks and the Fenton candlesticks. We not only have problems with the colors made, but the dates that each article shown was made. Because of this, we have elected to attribute the candlesticks shown as being produced at the Wheeling, West Virginia plant. The dates the Wheeling plant produced glass was from 1901 to 1926.

Shade Detail

Holder Detail

1&3. Stretch, 8½″ high.
Item 1 is shown with free-hole bobeche (held in place only by the candle). Colors: Stretch glass in apple green (shown), mint green (we may be showing mint green instead of apple green), blue, and amber. Current value, $36.00 - 42.00.

2. 3-Piece Candlestick Lamp - "Grapes", 10½″ high.
This is one of the rarest of all Northwood candlesticks. Rare because the shade was so easily broken. Also, if the metal candle/shade holder was damaged, it was usually thrown out and just the candlestick used. We are showing the shade and candle/shade holder to allow you a better perspective of this item. This item is mold marked as shown on the insert. Colors: green carnival (iridescent) shown. Other known colors are purple carnival (iridescent) — the rarest of colors, marigold carnival (iridescent) and green carnival. Can be found in plain olive green. Current value, $250.00 - 275.00.

4&5. 5-Rings, 8½″ high.
This is one of the last patterns made by Northwood (appeared in a late advertisement). Colors: Chinese red and blue stretch (shown), topaz, and russet iridescent. Current value, $38.00 - 44.00.

6. Hexagon Panels, 8½″ high. Also made 7″ high.
Colors: amber stretch (shown), lemon-yellow, and pink iridescent. There is a possibility it can be found in amethyst. Current value, $40.00 - 45.00.

7,8,9,10. No. 696, Item 7 10″ high and Items 8, 9, 10 8½″ high.
We have shown both the 8½″ and 10″ high to allow a better comparison in the variance of the two sizes. In other publications, we listed the jade as Fenton. On Plate 14, Items 4 & 6, we show these candlesticks with the Fenton No. 349 and No. 449. It is easy to wrongly identify these as you can see. Colors: Item 7 blue stretch, Item 8 & 10 jade green, Item 9 amber. Other known colors are plain green, blue, yellow Stretch and we believe plain yellow. Current value, $35.00 - 45.00.

1

2

3

4

5

6

7

8

9

10

Information note: When Paden City Glass Company closed in 1951, Canton Glass Company of Marion, Indiana bought their molds. Many of the Paden City candlesticks were then produced by Canton; yet, Canton continued to use the Paden City numbers. Therefore, we have not tried to separate the two. Where we have records and/or information which indicate that Canton also made a particular candlestick we will show an indication in the following manner: (CGC). Having no cut-off dates for the items, we will only list a circa for the basic time frame for the items.

1. No. 115, circa 1920's, 9″ high.
   Also made 7″ high. The most distinct difference in this candlestick and the ones shown on New Martinsville Plate 39, Items 1, 2, 4 & 5 and the one on Fostoria Plate 22, Item 1, is in the base — and of course the colors of New Martinsville. As we indicated with the other candlesticks, it has been difficult to unravel. We attributed this article to Paden City based on the notchings on the shaft (stem) of the candlestick. We have seen other items, identified to us as Paden City, with the same type notchings (cuttings). Paden City also used this item for other cuttings; example of this is cutting No. 113 — Floural Design. Current value, $18.00 - 22.00.

2. No. 117, circa 1920's, 8¼″ high.
   Colors: amber-gold striped decoration (shown), mulberry, green, blue, and black. Current value, $20.00 - 26.00.

3. No. 76 Tiffin.
   Shown for comparison. See U.S. Glass, Plate 51, Item 11 & 13 for details. Current value $22.00 - 28.00.

4. No. 109, circa 1920's, 9″ high.
   Colors: We are not aware of any other colors. Current value, $30.00 - 34.00.

5&10. No. 112, circa 1920's. Item 5. 8½″ high.
   Current value, $26.00 - 30.00. Item 10. 5½″ high. Also made 7″ high and 3½″ high. Current value, $12.00 - 14.00. Only made in crystal.

6. No. 220 Largo Line, circa 1930's, 5″ high.
   Most often confused with Cambridge "Caprice" line. This number and/or line indication may not be correct. Our information was a little vague but we felt sure it was Paden City. We have not seen this item in any other color. Current value, $12.00 - 16.00.

7. No. 113, circa 1920's, 3½″ high.
   Also made in 5½″, 7″ and 8½″ high. This is another pattern made by a number of glass houses. The size is the key to our identifying it as Paden City. We do not believe it was made in any other colors. The catalog showing this item did indicate that it was also made engraved and etched. We have yet to see either. Current value, $18.00 - 22.00.

8. No. 114, circa 1930's, 6½″ high.
   Also made 7″ high. Is it Paden City, Cambridge or Duncan? We took various items of this shape, checked all the details of each (sockets, hollow base indications, etc.) and placed them accordingly. Here the color and the notching on the stem are guides. Colors: amber (shown), blue green, possibly mulberry and black. Current value, $8.00 - 12.00.

9. No. 881 Line, circa 1930's, 6″ high.
   Was used for etchings. One example is P.E.553 — Irwin. Hazel Marie Weatherman referred to this pattern as the "Wotta Line." Current value, $16.00 18.00.

11. No. 215 (CGC), circa 1940-1960, 5″ high.
    We have no color listings. Current value, $10.00 - 12.00.

12. No. 900 Single (CGC), circa 1940-1960, 4½″ high.
    There is also a No. 900 "2-Way" (2-light), 6″ high. We have no color listings. Current value, $8.00 - 10.00.

13. No. 444 2-Way (CGC), circa 1940-1960, 5″ high.
    This item is usually confused with Imperial's No. 400/100-Twin, see Plate 30, Item 10. We have no color listings. Current value, $14.00 - 18.00.

14. No. 444 Single (CGC), circa 1940-1960, 6″ high.
    Flashed socket and base (applied color and fired into glass). We have not seen this item in any molded colors. Current value, $12.00 - 14.00.

15. No. 330 Single (CGC), circa 1920*-1960, 6½″ high.
    Frosted etching "Gadroon" on base. *Date based on etching on base. Difficult to see so we are showing it as an insert. We have no color listings. Current value, $16.00 - 20.00.

1

2

3

4

5

6

7

8

9

10

11

12

13

14

15

Paden City
Paden City Glass Manufacturing Company
1916-1951

1,2,3. No. 300 Line Console Set, circa 1925-1935, candlestick 3½″ high, bowl No. 5 shape, 14″, cutting unknown.
Colors: cheri-glo (shown), amber, green, and crystal. Current value Items 1 & 3, $12.00 - 16.00. Current value Item 2, $22.00 - 26.00.

4. No. 191 Party Line, circa 1928-1935, 3″ high.
Can be found with a "Step-ring" base as No. 192. Colors: crystal shown. Other known colors are cheri-glo, green and amber. We believe in later years possibly ruby and royal blue were added. Current value, $8.00 - 10.00.

5. No. 108 Plain, circa 1920, 4″ high.
We have no color listings. Current value, $6.00 - 8.00.

6. No. 108 Handled, circa 1920's, 4″ high.
We have no color listings. Current value, $8.00 - 10.00.

7. No. 412 Line Crows Foot Square, circa 1930's, 5½″ high.
This article was used for a number of etchings. A few were as follows: Trumpet Flower, Gothic Garden, Orchid, and Mrs. "B". Colors: ruby (red) as shown. Other known colors are opal, ebony, mulberry, cheri-glo, yellow, dark green, crystal and primrose. Current value, $18.00 - 22.00.

8,9,10. No. 555 Line "Nerva" Pattern, circa 1930's, 6″ high.

Item 8. Single with bobeche and ruby-flashed hurricane shade.

Shade is cut with grape pattern. Current value, $32.00 - 40.00.

Item 9. Single with etched base. Current value, $16.00 - 20.00.

Item 10. 2-Light. Current value, $20.00 - 24.00.

Colors: crystal shown. Ruby has been found in other items in the "Nerva" pattern, but we have no record that candlesticks were made in any colors.

11. No. 890 Line Crows Foot Round, 6½″ high.
We have no listing for colors for the Crow's Foot Round. The Crow's Foot Square should be a guide as most of the Crow's Foot patterns in other articles came in the colors listed above. Current value, $14.00 - 18.00.

1&5. No. 1600/Candle "Engraved Grapes", 12″ high.
Colors: cobalt blue and canaria (shown), light green, amethyst, and rosaria. There is a possibility that the grape design can be found in marina blue and auroria (amber). Current value, $60.00 - 85.00.

2,3,4. Console Set, sold with 4 candlesticks (2 not shown).
Candlesticks are 4″ high. Pairpoint also used this design with silver over-lay and/or silver painted design. Colors: cobalt with crystal bubble ball (shown). We have not seen any other color in the candlestick. We have seen the bowl in canaria and auroria; therefore, there is a possibility that the candlesticks exist in these colors also. Current value Items 2 & 4, $35.00 - 40.00. Current value Item 3, $100.00 - 125.00.

6. No. 1600/Candle "Colias" Pattern, 13″ high.
Colors: auroria (shown), light green, crystal and possibly canaria. Current value, $120.00 - 130.00.

7. Twist Base-Smoke Top, 3½″ high.
Gundersen-Pairpoint . We have no listings of the other colors; however, there is a possible chance that it may be found with a ruby top (based on the theory that smoke top is applied color and Gundersen applied ruby tops to a number of this type item). Current value, $28.00 - 32.00.

8. Cobalt, 4½″ high.
Shown only to illustrate that variance in size with the console set above. Current value, $40.00 - 45.00.

9. Paper Weight Candle, 4″ high.
Believed to be Gundersen-Pairpoint. The same theory applies as Item 7, Gundersen applies color tops (sockets) to this type item. A lot of bubble items made by Erickson Glass Works are confused with Pairpoint and Gundersen-Pairpoint Glass. The basic answer is left up to the design. Current value, $30.00 - 34.00.

10. No. B 1627/Candle, 10″ high.
Can be found with "Dew Drop" design engraving and Wexford. Colors: amethyst with crystal bubble shown. Other known colors are cobalt, marina blue, rosenia, canaria, auroria and light green. Current value, $45.00 - 50.00.

11. No. 1600/Candle "Cornwall" Design engraved, 12″ high.
Colors: crystal shown. We believe that it can be found in auroria, light green, and canaria. Current value, $90.00 - 100.00.

12,13,14. No. 1642/Candle (bowl no. unknown), 4″ high.
Was also used for engraving. One known usage was the "Wilton" Design. Colors: auroria shown. We have no listings for any other colors. Current value, $30.00 - 55.00.

15. No. 1600/Candle "Hampton" Design engraved. 12″ high.
We have been fortunate to be able to show you four patterns using the No. 1600/Candle shape candlestick. Other major design engravings using the No. 1600/Candle are as follows: Old Colony Design, Coronal Design, Rockford Pattern, Victoria Design, Waterford Design and Wiltin Design. We have no record, but believe that it was used for Nottingham Pattern, Dew Drop Pattern and Veneti Design. Colors: Crystal shown. Probably can be found in auroria, light green and canaria. Current value, $90.00 - 100.00.

1

2

3

4

5

6

7

8

9

10

11

12

13

14

15

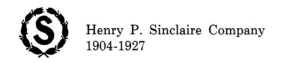

Henry P. Sinclaire Company
1904-1927

1. No. 2914, circa 1920-1927, 9″ high.
   Light amber shown. We have no listing for other colors. Current value, $32.00 - 38.00.

2. No. 2900 Cut Panels, circa 1920-1927, 9″ high.
   Amber shown. We have no listing for other colors. Current value, $65.00 - 75.00.

3,4,5. Blanks, circa 1920-1927.
   These blanks are shown as Sinclaire only because Sinclaire listed the shape "For-Sale" as blanks. They could very well be No. 1600/Candle Blanks made by Pairpoint. Now here is where confusion creeps in; It is our understanding that Sinclaire bought some blanks from Pairpoint, Steuben and we know of one vase from Fostoria. Item 5 was obtained in New Bedford, Mass., as a Pairpoint blank, yet we have found no listing for a 14″ No. 1600/Candle, therefore, we have shown it as Sinclaire.

   Item 3. No. 340, 10″ high, light green. Current value, $34.00 - 42.00.

   Item 4. No. 3402, 12″ high, amethyst. Current value, $40.00 - 50.00.

   Item 5. No. 3402, 14″ high, crystal. Current value, $50.00 - 60.00.

6. No. 3401 (cutting pattern unknown), circa 1920's, 9″ high.
   We have no other listing for colors. Current value, $18.00 - 24.00.

7&8. No. 12902, circa 1920-1927, 9″ high.
   We believe that this item was also No. 2925.

   Item 7. Crystal with engraved cutting. Current value, $30.00 - 34.00.

   Item 8. Elfin green with prisms. This item is signed with trade-mark. Current value, $40.00 - 45.00.

   Other known colors are amber and colonia blue.

9. No. 12928, circa 1920-1927, 3½″ high.
   We have no listing of colors. Current value, $22.00 - 28.00.

10,11,12. No. 12900, circa 1920-1927, 10″ and 12″ high shown.
   Also made 8″ and 15″ high. Can also be found with prisms in the 10″ and 12″. Colors: amber and colonia blue (shown), amethyst, and elfin green. Current value, $75.00 - 100.00.

1

2

3

4

5

6

7

8

9

10

11

12

The following Steuben plates are devoted to glass manufactured before a major policy change by Corning-Steuben Division: to make only clear crystal and no colored glass. We have established this date as about 1933. We have shown four pieces of the New Steuben (as it is called) to allow a comparison between the "old" and the "new". We have been unable to list production numbers for the New Steuben, only because we have spent no time in trying to research them. The Old Steuben has been difficult enough!

1,2,3,6. New Steuben clear crystal.
Notice that the base of the console set bowl and Item 6 base are the same design. Current value Items 1 & 3, $850.00 - 950.00. Current value Item 2, $1400.00 - 1600.00. Current value Item 6, $85.00 - 105.00.

4&8. No. 3369, 12″ high.
Pale green threaded bobeche, pale green base rim, twist stem with green knobs. Current value, $150.00 - 170.00.

5. 2940, 8½″ high.
Dark amethyst twisted stem, amber topez socket and base. Can also be found with celeste blue stem and amber topez socket and base. Current value, $100.00 - 125.00.

7. Swirl-low, 3½″ high.
We have shown this as a Steuben because of the general make-up of the glass. It has all the "ear-marks" of a Steuben, but we cannot find a listing; therefore, we present it with reservations. Colors: pale green. Current value, $55.00 - 60.00.

9,10,11. No. 6045 Console Set, shown with No. 6044 bowl — centerpiece.
12″ high candlesticks. Colors: pamona green stem, amber swirl base and socket. Current value, $160.00 - $190.00.

1

2

3

4

5

6

7

8

9

10

11

1. No. 6506, 14″ high.
    Colors: French blue. Current value, $150.00 - 160.00.

2&3. No. 3315, 18″ high.
    Yes, there is a larger Steuben candlestick — No. 3397, 20″ high. Colors: jade green. Current value, $300.00 - 400.00.

4,5,6,7. No. 2956, 10″ and 12″ high shown.
    We believe that this pattern was used more than any other candlestick.

Item 4. Flint white stem, light jade blue base and socket. This candlestick has a metal candle holder in socket. Metal candle holder is removable. 12″ high. Current value, $185.00 - 220.00.

Item 5. Amber topaz. 12″ high. Current value, $175.00 - 200.00.

Item 6. Celeste blue. 10″ high. Current value, $180.00 - 200.00.

Item 7. Amber topaz stem, flemish blue base and socket. 12″ high. Current value, $190.00 - 225.00.

Other known colors are gold ruby cased over crystal and cut — very rare; amber topaz stem, dark amethyst base and socket; flint white stem, jade green base and socket; black with engraved Indian pattern; and aqua marine. We feel sure this is just a few that were used.

8,9,10. No. 6110 Console Set, bowl No. 3579.
    The fruit in the bowl is glass and alabaster. Current value Items 8 & 10, $200.00 - 230.00. Current value Item 9, $250.00 - 300.00.

1

2

3

4

5

6

7

8

9

10

Teardrop candlesticks • Height 9" • $100.00 a

Crystal candlesticks—for a brilliant table

STEUBEN GLASS ❄

Ad for Steubenglass from the April 18, 1964, New Yorker.

1. No. 6043, 12" high.
   Colors: celeste blue with mica flecks stem, amber topaz socket and base. Current value, $175.00 - 200.00.

2,3,4. No. 5194 Console Set, 10" high candlesticks, No. 7023 bowl.
   Colors: celeste blue. Current value Items 2 & 4, $250.00 - 275.00. Current value Item 3, $350.00 - 400.00.

5. No. 196 Verre De Soie, 10" high.
   Including Items 2 and 4 above, there are 6 basic Steuben patterns using this stem twist. Colors: verre de soie. Current value, $160.00 - 180.00.

6,7,8. No. 6384, 4" high
   Item 6. Pamona Green — Plain. Current value, $45.00 - 60.00.
   Item 7. Yellow Canary — Twist. Current value, $50.00 - 65.00.
   Item 8. Topaz-Panel. Current value, $50.00 - 65.00.

9&10. Reeded socket — gold (pattern no. unknown), 3" high.
   Crystal, random bubbles in base, reeded (hand applied threading) gold socket. Current value, $70.00 - 80.00.

11&13. Reeded base and socket (pattern no. unknown), 6" high.
   Colors: French blue. Current value, $65.00 - 75.00.

12. No. 5114, 11" high.
   Colors: yellow canary. Current value, $75.00 - 90.00.

Plate 48

United States Glass Company
1891-Present
Tiffin Crystal-Division of Towle Silversmiths Corp.

Plate No. 49

1&5. No. 66 Twist, 7½" high.

The twists have been a research problem for years. At first, collectors, including us, attributed all of the twists (No. 66 pattern) to Cambridge. Then doubts began to creep into our thinking. Now we feel that the twists are "un-twisted." First, we ask you to read the write-up of Plate 6, Items 8, 9, 10, 11 & 12. Of the five twists shown, four are U.S. Glass and one is Cambridge. Another interesting point, check the height of these candlesticks. They range from 7½" high to 8½" high. We stated two important differences between the Cambridge twist and the No. 66 U.S. Glass twist. Now let's add a third difference — height. U.S. Glass lists only a 7½" size, but we know this varies from about 8¼" down. The Cambridge is 8½" high (plus or minus). Now, we leave you with one major problem — color. We have listed a few that we have information on, but there are probably many more not listed. Therefore, when in doubt, check your mold-marks (seams): three for U.S. Glass, two for Cambridge.

Colors: Item 1. tomato. Current value, $28.00 - 32.00. Item 5. decorated, blue body, dark blue base. band with gold enameled flowers and leaves (on clear crystal) shown. Current value, $22.00 - 26.00. Colors shown on the Cambridge plate are the two above (Items 8 & 9) and Item 10 — carmal, Item 12 — black satin. Other known colors are ambrina, watermelon (red-to-green-to-red), green satin and canary satin. Possibly in plain glass in light blue, canary, amber and light green.

Known decorated colors on clear crystal blanks or white satin are as follows: "Esmeralda" — decorated butter cup, green band, gold lines, enameled flowers and leaves, circa 1926-1935. "Miami" — decorated wilk rose with gold (hand painted), circa 1926-1935. "Madrid" — decorated red body, black border and red panel with gold print and scroll, circa 1926-1929. Other usage was cut decorations such as pattern "Meridian", circa 1924-1937.

2,3,4. No. 15179 Bell-twist Console Set, candlesticks 9" high.

We still do not have a production (catalog) number for the candlesticks. The bowl is No. 315, 7½" high foot comport. Canary satin shown. For other colors see Items 1 & 5 above. Current value, $32.00 - 42.00.

6&9 No. 10 Helio pattern, circa 1910-1950, 1½" high.

Why this item was used so extensively we do not know. The fact that so many companies made one like it has got to be as much a mystery as the popularity of the item. We have listed five other glass houses that used this basic style. They are as follows: Fenton, Pattern No. 314, circa 1915-1925; Cambridge, Pattern No. 227½, circa 1930; Duncan-Miller, Pattern No. 35, circa 1920-1930; L.E. Smith, Pattern No. 110, "By Cracky", circa 1930; Bartlett-Collins, Pattern No. 87, circa 1927. Colors: white satin with scroll decorations shown. Other known colors, both in bright (plain) and satin finish are blue, green, canary, amber, pink, black and crystal. Decorated patterns were as follows: "Minton" design — gold encrusted, "Autumn Leaf" — hand decorated on pink blanks only (very colorful), "Bruxelles" — lace satin design, gold trimmings on pink and green blanks. Current value, $8.00 - 10.00.

1674   THE POTTERY GAZETTE AND GLASS TRADE REVIEW.   *November 1, 1922.*

Autumn Announcement

WE ARE FEATURING A NOTEWORTHY DISPLAY OF DECORATED LINES & NOVELTIES IN TABLE GLASSWARE & SPECIAL SHAPES IN CANDLESTICKS IN OUR SHOWROOMS~ CALL & SEE US~OR WRITE ~AND GET INTO TOUCH *NOW* WITH VOGUE PRODUCTIONS FOR NINETEEN TWENTY-THREE ~~~~

UNITED STATES GLASS CO
55 FARRINGDON ST LONDON EC4
TELEPHONE CENTRAL 5861

1   2   3   4   5

6   7   8   9

10   11   12   13   14

7&8.   "Puritan", circa 1926-1931, 3″ high.
Decoration on crystal-satined blank. We have no other color information. Current value, $14.00 - 16.00.

10.   No. 82, circa 1924-1934, 8½″ high.
Colors: blue satin with silver overlay. Other known colors are black satin, canary satin, green satin, red satin, bright red and bright green. Current value, $35.00 - 40.00.

11,12,13.   No. 76 Console Set, circa 1924-1935, candlestick 8½″ high with No. 330 candy jar and cover.

Colors: flowers enameled on crystal satin blanks. Other known colors are crystal clear blanks, white satin blanks and royal blue satin blanks.

Known decorated blanks are as follows: "Pekin" — decorated with red band, black print, ivory background on clear crystal blank. "Esmeralda" — decorated with butter cup, green band, gold lines, enameled flowers and leaves on clear crystal blank. "Gold Line Decoration No. 1" — on royal blue satin blank. "Miami" — decorated wild rose on gold on white satin blank. Current value, $22.00 - 34.00.

14.   No. 127-510 Modern Candelabra, circa 1950's, 7½″ high.
Also made 9½″ & 11½″ high. We named this "Modern Candelabra" because the advertisement we have showed it with a shade that fits in the socket cup. Colors: plum shown. Also made in golden banana. Current value, $18.00 - 20.00.

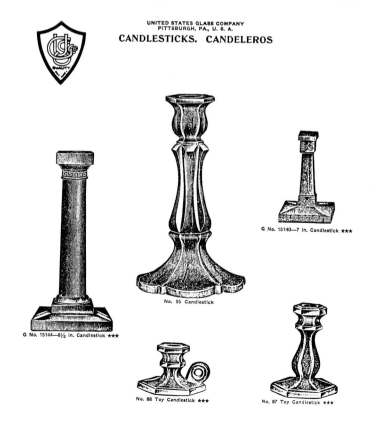

The "G" before the candlestick number is an indication that the item was made at Factory "G", Glassport, Pa.

1919 Sales Catalog.

CANDLESTICKS. CANDELEROS

No.61 CANDLESTICK
(CUT TOP & BOTTOM)

No.51 CANDLESTICK
(CUT TOP & BOTTOM)

No.50 CANDLESTICK
(CUT TOP & BOTTOM)

No.52 CANDLESTICK
(CUT TOP & BOTTOM)

1919 SALES CATALOG "F" FACTORY
(OLD RIPLEY & COMPANY, PITTSBURGH)

1&5. No. 151, circa 1924-1934, 9" high.
Notice difference between Item 1 and 5. Most likely Item 5 is either a re-worked mold or a totally different mold using the same number. Could also be that one was made at the Tiffin, Ohio plant and the other at any one of the other plant locations. See Plate 51, Items 10, 11 & 12 console set for additional coverage. Colors: bright black with gold line decoration. Current value, $18.00 - 22.00.

2,3,4. No. 15328 Brilliancy Console Set, circa 1926-1930's.
C onsists of: No. 15328 candlestick — 8" high and No. 15328 console bowl — rolled edge. It is important to notice the similiar shapes of this item and No. 151 beside it. Colors: amber shown. Other known colors are light blue, canary and light green. Current value, $20.00 - 35.00.

6. No. 63, circa 1924-1934, 7½" high.
Colors: blue decorated on clear crystal blank. Other known colors are clear crystal blanks, red on clear crystal blanks, black satin, ivory on clear crystal blanks. Current value, $10.00 - 12.00.

7,8,9,10. No. 17 Small-Handled, circa 1926-1939, 1½" high.
Colors: crystal and green (shown), blue. Current values, $12.00 - 18.00.

11. No. 77, circa 1926-1929, 7" high.
Colors: red decorated on clear crystal blank (shown), clear crystal blank, blue decorated on clear crystal blank, and green on clear crystal blank. One other listing shows it with "Madrid" decoration — red body, black border and red panel, gold print and scroll on clear crystal blank. Current value, $10.00 - 12.00.

12&16. No. 9758 "Flanders" etching shown, circa 1914-1935, 3½" high.
The etched "Flanders" Design was one of the oldest etched patterns made by U.S. Glass. The unique things about this pair of candlesticks are the bobeches and prisms. Both are pink and very difficult to find. The bobeches are free-holes (held in place only by the candle) and are easily broken. Colors: rose (pink) (shown), crystal, mandarin-crystal trim, and rose-crystal trim. Current value, $22.00 - 28.00.

Other patterns and colors (etched designs): "Persian Pheasant" — all crystal, crystal-green trim and rose. Circa 1930-1935. "Minton" — gold encrusted on 188 line, regular optic, all rose, matt finish also 196 line, wide optic, all crystal, matt finish. Circa 1930's. "Floris" — all crystal, crystal-green trim and all rose. Circa 1927-1935. "Fontaine" — crystal-green trim, all twilite, all rose, twilite-crystal trim. Circa 1924-1931. "Modernistic" — all green and all rose. Circa 1925-1935. "Psyche" — crystal-green trim. Circa 1926-1931. "Vogue" — all crystal, all green, all rose. Circa 1926-1931.

Other patterns and colors (cut designs): Cut "413", rock crystal, circa 1924-1935; Cut "414", rock crystal, circa 1924-1936; Cut "421", rock crystal, circa 1924-1936; Cut "Green Wheat", crystal-green trim. circa 1924-1936; Cut "405", all crystal and all rose, circa 1930-1935; Cut "416", rock crystal, circa 1929-1936; Cut "417", rock crystal, circa 1930-1935; Cut "418", rock crystal, circa 1929-1934; Cut "424", all mandarin, circa 1929-1934; Cut "Moritz", rock crystal, circa 1929-1936.

1   2   3   4   5

6   7   8   9   10   11

12   13   14   15   16

Lancelot pattern, introduced in 1949.

13&15. No. 348 "Juno" etching, circa 1926-1933, 4″ high.
Colors: topaz shown. Other known colors are green, pink, and crystal. We have only one listing for other etched patterns: "Oneida", circa 1927-1935. Was also furnished with platinum band. Cut patterns known were N-Cut "Scinfra" (polished), and "Stareath" (gray), both on rock crystal. Current value, $18.00 - 24.00.

14. No. 5831 2-Light Candelabrum, circa 1930, 6″ high.
Colors: crystal with "June" cutting shown. Other known colors are green, mandarin, rose and crystal — plain. Current value, $20.00 - 26.00.

Etched patterns and colors: "Ansonia" — all crystal and mandarin-crystal trim. Circa 1930's. "Dalton" — all crystal and mandarin-crystal trim. Circa 1930's. "Harw" — all crystal and mandarin-crystal trim. Circa 1930-1934. "La Salle" — all crystal and crystal-mandarin trim. Circa 1932-1935. "Navarre" — all crystal and mandarin-crystal trim. Circa 1932-1935. "Rosalind" — all crystal and all mandarin. Circa 1932-1935.

Cut patterns on crystal are: Cut "447" — "Beverly", circa 1929-1935; Cut "448" — "Belmont", circa 1932-1936; N-Cut "Scinfra" (polished), circa 1934; "Stareath" (gray), circa 1934

Other patterns on crystal-platinum encrusted: "Leaf-Byzantine", circa 1932-1937; "Rose-Helena", circa 1930-1936.

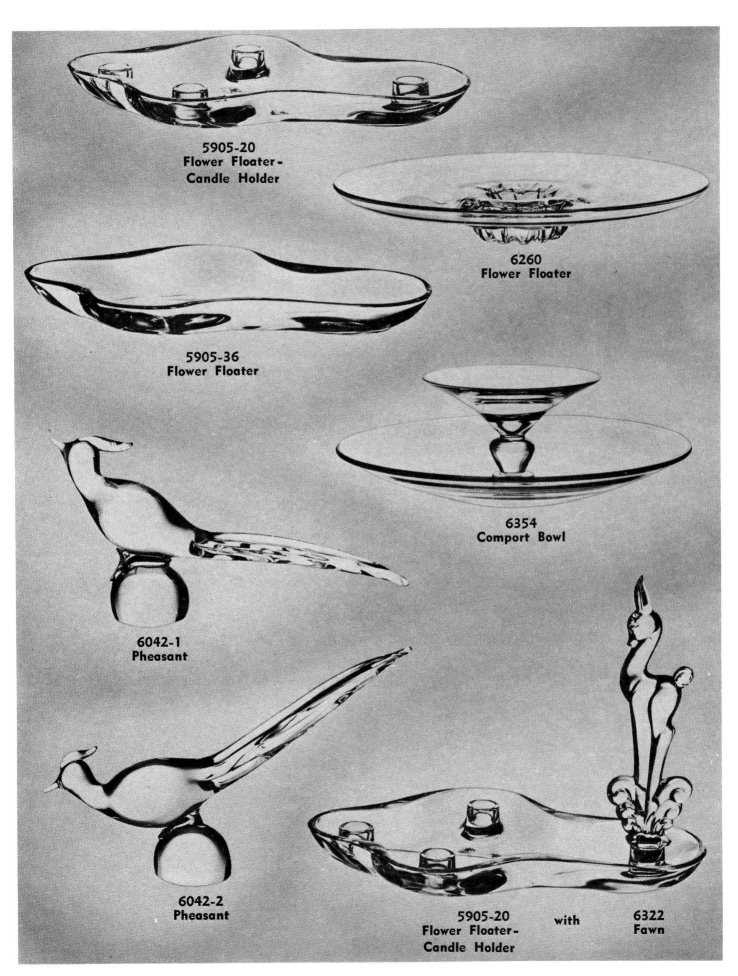

5905-20
Flower Floater -
Candle Holder

6260
Flower Floater

5905-36
Flower Floater

6354
Comport Bowl

6042-1
Pheasant

6042-2
Pheasant

5905-20   **with**   **6322**
Flower Floater-   **Fawn**
Candle Holder

The FLOWER FLOATER W/FAWN was introduced in the late 1940's in cyrstal, Copan blue and Citron green. It was the product of the creative genius of two Tiffin Glassmasters—John Fleming and Paul Hoover.

1&3. No. 75, circa 1924-1934, 9½" high.
Colors: bright black, green (shown), black, satin, blue, amber and crystal. Current value, $28.00 - 32.00

2. "Flower Floater" with Fawn, circa 1940-1950's.
Colors: topaz (shown), copen blue, and citron green. We also think that it can be found in twilite, which if found, should be considered very rare. Current value, $65.00 - 85.00. There are two other configurations of the "Flower Floater" with Fawn. One is "Boat" shaped with a candle holder at one end, fawn and fawn holder shaped like the one shown three candle holders on one end, one candle holder on the opposite and a fawn and fawn holder on the side.

4. No. 15319, Baluster, circa 1923-1936, 8" high.
In the 1920's, the number was changed to No. 319. Also No. 319-202, gold rubber stamp design on black satin blands. Etched pattern "Brocade" on bright black was made 1924-1934. Colors: Ink satin shown. Other known colors are bright red, bright green, blue, canary, green, red, black satin and pink. Baseline was listed, but this may be the same as canary. Current value, $35.00 - 40.00

5. No. 345, Low, circa 1923-1935, 2½" high.
Gold encrusted "Athens" Design shown. Colors: rose (pink) shown. Other known colors are crystal and green. Other known patterns etched are: "Lois" — green and pink, circa 1923-1935, "Trojan" — crystal and green, circa 1926-1932, current value, $10.00 - 14.00.

6&7. No. 18 Low, circa 1926-1939, 2" high.
Colors: amber satin and bright crystal (shown), blue, green, canary, pink, black and crystal. Candlestick appears to have color; it does, but not as one would expect. It is suncolored, also known as sun purpled glass, turned glass, amethystine glass or desert glass. As we stated in the Cambridge section, the color is caused by the use of manganese in the glass as a decolorizing agent and the item being subjected to direct sunlight. The color change could take from 2 to 10 years to reach a maximum depth of color. This article was given to us by Glenna and Arnold Preheim of Anaheim, California (former owners of the Purple Glass Farm, Anaheim). When their shop was operating, it was devoted to sun-turned glass. Current value, $6.00 - 10.00.

8. No. 79, circa 1922-1934, 6" high.
Colors: dark green shown. We only have records to verify ruby, black satin, and bright black, but the transparent color shown leads us to believe that this item was made in many colors. Black Glass was as follows: "Satin Ribbon" decoration furnished on black glass. "Brocade" Pattern on bright black glass "Kimberly" Pattern on ruby glass. Current value, $10.00 - 14.00.

1

2

3

4

5

6

7

8

9

10

11

12

13

Good Housekeeping,
November, 1924

9. No. 82, circa 1924-1934, 8½″ high.
Colors: blue (shown), crystal, green, amber, canary, white satin, and black satin. Known decorations are as follows: "Miami" decorated, wild rose and gold on white satin blanks. "Esmeralda" decorated, butter cup, green band, gold lines, enameled flowers and leaves on clear crystal blanks. "Madrid" decorated, red body, black border and red panel, gold print and scroll on clear crystal blanks. Current value, $26.00 - 34.00.

10,11,12. No. 151, Console Set, circa 1924-1934, 9″ high.
Colors: decorated, green shade with gold encrusted on clear crystal blanks. We believe gold encrusted band to be "Minton" design. We do not have a total color listing. Current value, $22.00 - 36.00

13. No. 15310, circa 1922-1935, 9″ high.
In 1920's changed number to No. 310. Colors: clear crystal blanks shown. Other known colors are Holly Satin Assortment (green and red satin finish), bright or satin finish furnished in green, pink and black. Used also for "Mercer" cut assortment. Current value, $20.00 - 26.00

THE TIFFIN DOLPHIN

While researching my soon to be released book of the *Tiffin Glassmaster* series, I discovered in a lamp catalogue of the U.S. Glass Company, dated 1928, a dolphin candlestick which was being advertised as a lamp base. The U.S. Glass Company (Factory R) of Tiffin, OH furnished the base only, with a metal cap for attaching the lamp socket.

This item was first made at the U.S. Glass Company's Glassport, PA plant but they experienced difficulties with the satin finishing of the items so the tooling was moved to Factory R.

This is the first time the dolphin candlestick of Tiffin Glass has been documented. It was produced in pink, green and crystal with transparent or satin finish. It is 8″ tall.

A two-piece fish bowl was also shown with a dolphin base - available in amber, blue, green, black, crystal or canary in transparent or satin finish.

These pieces have been seen at sales in the past, but I had no idea they were a product of Tiffini Glass.

The Tiffini dolphin candlestick has a round base and candle holder, where the Sandwich candlestick has a ruffled candle holder with a single or double step base. The Westmoreland dolphin candlestick is a reproduction of the Sandwich original as Westmoreland has mentioned in their advertisements.

I would appreciate hearing from any of you who are fortunate to own either of these dolphin items made by Tiffin.

GLASS REVIEW APRIL 1981

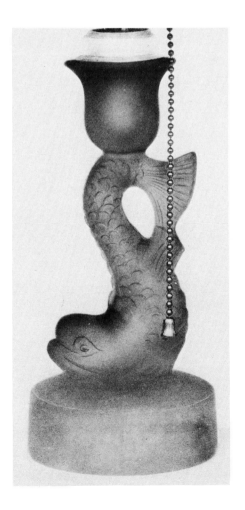

Tiffin
Glassmasters

BY FRED BICKENHEUSER

Price per Dozen, Crystal, Satin Finish 11.00
Price per Dozen, Green, Satin Finish 11.80
Price per Dozen, Pink, Satin Finish 12.50
Carton to hold 3 Dozen .... 50¢ Each

Note; - We furnish the Standard only, with a white metal cap, for attaching
the socket. We do not furnish Socket, Cord, Plug or Shade.

We stated earlier, usually one type of glass or one pattern carried a glass house through trying times. This is the case of Tiffin black satin glass. It is recognizable by sight, and most of all, touch. Although we have repeated items on this plate, we felt that these were important to show together for comparison.

1,2,3.   No. 315, Console Set, circa 1924-1934, 9″ high. bowl, No. 15179, 10″ L.V. Comport.
Current value items 1 & 3, $25.00 - 30.00. Current value item 2, $35.00 - 45.00.

4.   No. 151, circa 1924-1934, 9″ high.
Notice the paper label on this article (U.S.G. Co.) Current value, $22.00 - 30.00.

5&6.   No. 326, Low, circa 1926-1939, 3½″ high.
Current value, $10.00 - 12.00

7.   Gold Line Decoration, circa 1924-1934, 9″ high.

Current value, $32.00 - 38.00

8,9,10.   No. 315, Console Set, Candlestick 9″ high.
bowl, No. 8076 10″ open work berry bowl and base. Current value items 8 & 10, $25.00 - 30.00.
Current value item 9, $45.00 - 50.00

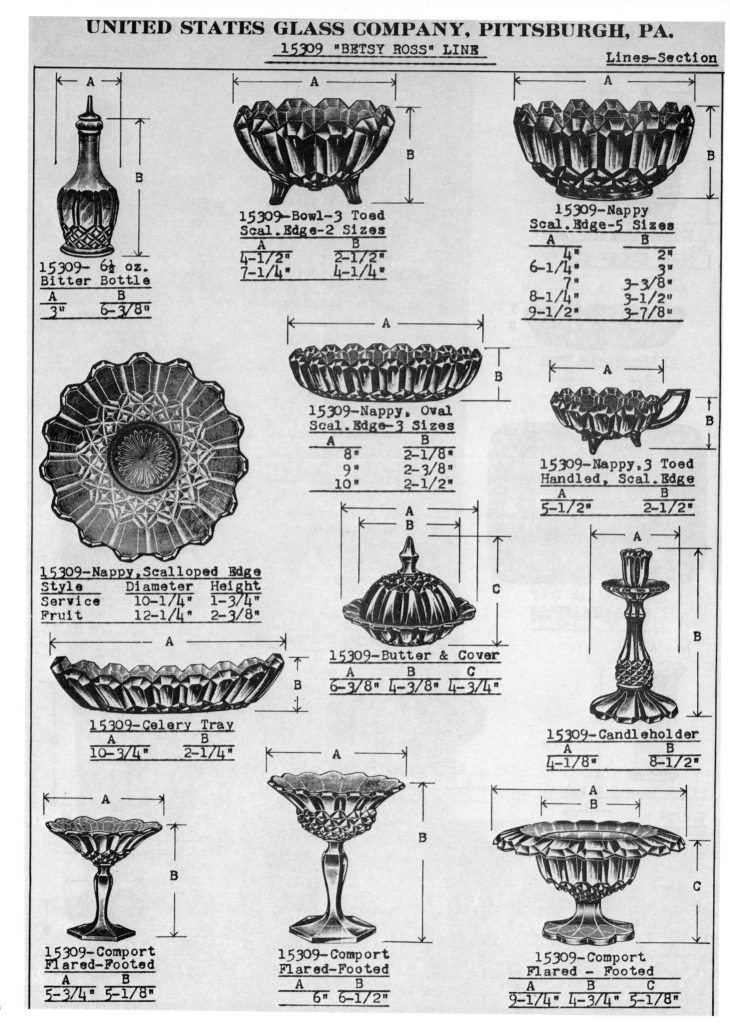

15309- 6½ oz. Bitter Bottle

A	B
3"	6-3/8"

15309-Bowl-3 Toed Scal.Edge-2 Sizes

A	B
4-1/2"	2-1/2"
7-1/4"	4-1/4"

15309-Nappy Scal.Edge-5 Sizes

A	B
4"	2"
6-1/4"	3"
7"	3-3/8"
8-1/4"	3-1/2"
9-1/2"	3-7/8"

15309-Nappy, Oval Scal.Edge-3 Sizes

A	B
8"	2-1/8"
9"	2-3/8"
10"	2-1/2"

15309-Nappy,3 Toed Handled, Scal.Edge

A	B
5-1/2"	2-1/2"

15309-Nappy,Scalloped Edge

Style	Diameter	Height
Service	10-1/4"	1-3/4"
Fruit	12-1/4"	2-3/8"

15309-Butter & Cover

A	B	C
6-3/8"	4-3/8"	4-3/4"

15309-Candleholder

A	B
4-1/8"	8-1/2"

15309-Celery Tray

A	B
10-3/4"	2-1/4"

15309-Comport Flared-Footed

A	B
5-3/4"	5-1/8"

15309-Comport Flared-Footed

A	B
6"	6-1/2"

15309-Comport Flared - Footed

A	B	C
9-1/4"	4-3/4"	5-1/8"

8842
Pin Wheel Coaster

115-122*
2 Light Candlestick
6½″ High x 7″ Wide

115-121*
1 Light Candlestick
3″ High

*Also available in Copen Blue, Citron Green and
Desert Red

153-110*
3 Pc. Garden Set
(2 #153-121 One Light Candlesticks—1 #153-98 Ash Tray)

*Also available in Copen Blue, Cit-
ron Green and Desert Red

This glass was made from Duncan-Miller molds obtained by U.S. Glass in 1955.

Tiffin modern era of the 1950's.

Tiffin modern era of the 1950's.

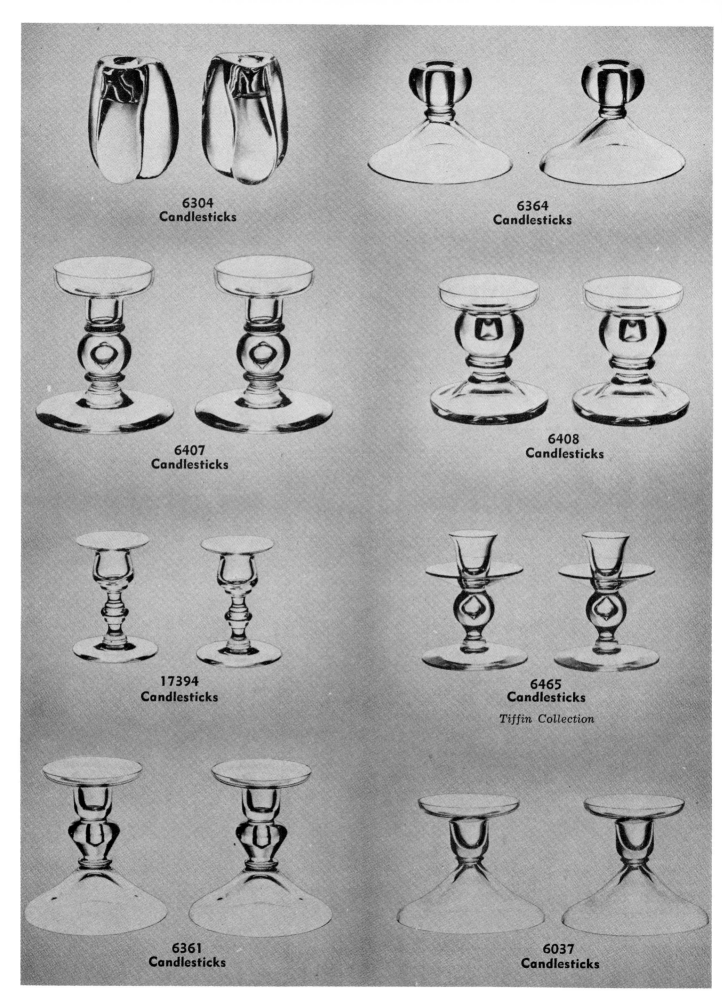

6304
Candlesticks

6364
Candlesticks

6407
Candlesticks

6408
Candlesticks

17394
Candlesticks

6465
Candlesticks

Tiffin Collection

6361
Candlesticks

6037
Candlesticks

1951 Tiffin Catalog.

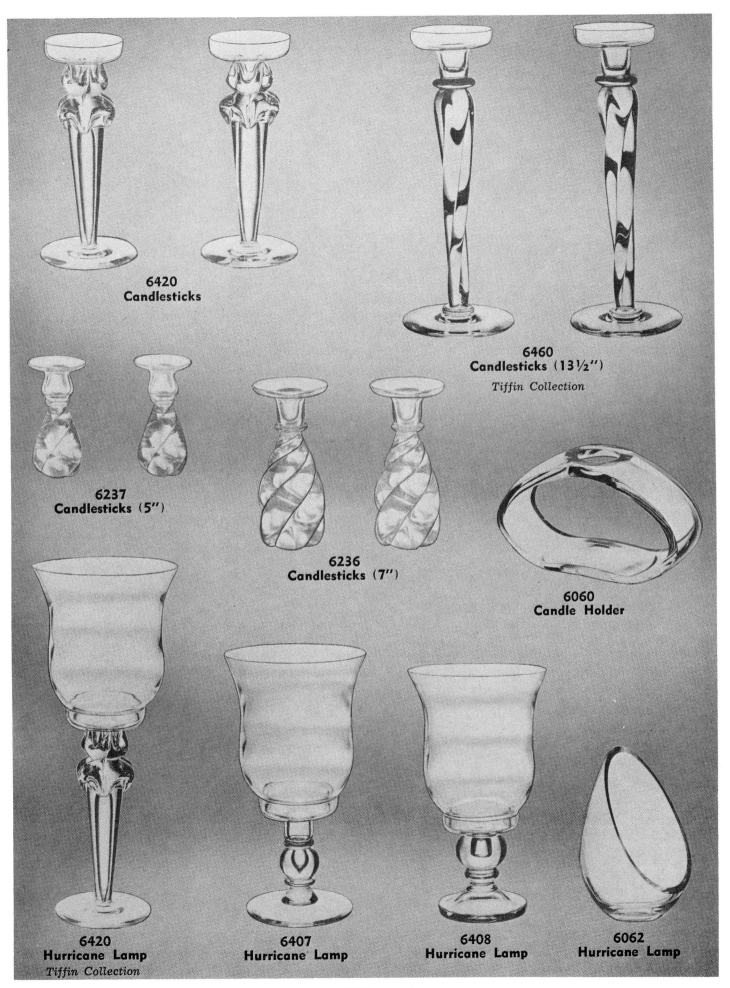

6420
Candlesticks

6460
Candlesticks (13½″)

Tiffin Collection

6237
Candlesticks (5″)

6236
Candlesticks (7″)

6060
Candle Holder

6420
Hurricane Lamp
Tiffin Collection

6407
Hurricane Lamp

6408
Hurricane Lamp

6062
Hurricane Lamp

1951 Tiffin catalog.

1. No. 1803, circa 1924-1930, 9″ high.
   Colors: decorated, blue stem, gold with webb lines and black rims on clear crystal blank; amber, green, rose (Roselin pink), and crystal. This item was used with many decorations (fired-on and hand-painted). Current value, $28.00 - 30.00

2,3,4,6,7. No. 1049, Dolphins, circa 1924-1935, 9″ and 4″ high.
   Dophin Comport is No. 1820 9″ high. Colors: green (shown), amber, blue, crystal and milk glass. 4″ high Colors: milk glass, and rose pink (shown), amber, green, blue and crystal. Milk glass first made in 1950's. Also you must *be aware* of reproduction of the 9″ size. The reproductions are in blue milk glass and shaded blue milk glass (frosted on edges). Current value items 2 & 4, $45.00 - 50.00. Current value item 3, $50.00 - 60.00. Current value items 6 & 7, $8.00 - 10.00.

5. No. 1933, circa 1940-1970, 6¾″ high.
   Colors: milk glass (shown), black, amber, and moss green. Current value, $18.00 - 20.00

8. No. 1017, circa 1920-1970, 8″ high.
   This article was also used as a lamp base in 1924. Colors: crystal (shown), rose (roselin), green, blue and amber. Current value, $16.00 - 20.00

9. Spoke and Rim (Number unknown), circa 1950-1960's, 3½″ high.
   Colors: moss green (shown), black, amber, and milk glass. Current value, $14.00 - 16.00

SPOKE AND RIM CONSOLE SET in hand-made black glass. Candlesticks, 3½ inches high, retail for about $3.90 a pair; hand-painted footed flared bowl, 11 inches wide, retails for about $10. Westmoreland Glass Company, Grapeville, Pa.

September, 1954, China, Glass & Tablewares.

GOOD HOUSEKEEPING
DECEMBER 1924

Left, charming glass candlesticks, dolphin design, 9″ high, in amber, green, or blue, $8 a pair. Oval oil flower painting, burnished gold frame, 19″ long, $10

Christmas Shopping Service

1

2

3

4

5

6

7

8

9

10

11

12

13

14

15

16

10&11.   No. 1067, Balls, circa 1924-1956, 2″ high.
         This item, when first issued in the early 1920's, had a round flat base on it. The base was about 5″ in diameter (rare). Colors: crystal with "flashed" color red and blue with socket and one ball crystal. Other known colors (flashed only) are ruby and blue, all surfaces coated. Current value, $20.00 - 24.00

12,14,16.   No. 1921, Low "Lotus", circa 1924-1975, 3″ high.
         We have shown three items to allow you to see the various treatments used on the bases. Item 12, a gift to us in 1975, has a full cup base. This item can be turned up-side-down and used as a nut bowl. Item 14 semi-flat and item 16 is flat. Item 16 depicts the low "Lotus" as it was issued in 1924. In fact, the catalog pictured it much flatter than shown. Colors: Item 12, amber satin, Item 14, decorated and fired-orange. Item 16, light blue-green (early blue). The only other color we have listed is rose (Roselin). Current value, $18.00 - 22.00.

13&15.   No. 1921, "Lotus" Tall, circa 1924-1930, 9″ high.
         Colors: crystal with gold fleck shown. Other known colors are amber, green, early blue (blue green) and rose (roselin). Current value, $35.00 - 40.00

WESTMORELAND GLASS COMPANY, Grapeville, Pa. Handmade milk glass Console Group reproduced from an old mold; bell-shaped bowl and candlesticks have all-over "Leaf" design. Bowl retails for about $5, candlesticks for about $5 a pair.

Suggested References

Specialty books, such as this are usually researched from basic reference material (publication, research papers, magazines, trade papers, and one of the best, collector club's publications). As we indicated in our "Foreword", the reference publications are the "tools" that made this book possible. Therefore, we are listing a number of publications that could improve your reference material. It should be understood, that we did not necessarily use these publications for the information in this text, but they have been a great help in the identification of much of our own collection;

General Listings (Covering Multi-Glass Houses)

The Collector's Encyclopedia of Depression Glass, Gene Florence, Collector Books, P.O. Box 3009, Paducah, Ky. 42001

Glass Review (Monthly) P.O. Box 542 Marietta, Ohio 45750

Depression Glass III, Sandra McPhee Stout, Wallace-Homestead Book Co. Des Moines, Iowa 50304

Iridescent Stretch Glass, Kitty & Russell Umbraco P.O. Box 1234 Berkeley, Calif.

Colored Glass of the Depression Era and *Colored Glass of the Depression Era-2*, Hazel Marie Weatherman, P.O. Box 4444 Springfield, Mo. 65804

American Glass, George S. & Helen McKearin, Crown Publishers, New York.

Stretch Glass, Berry Wiggins, Green Publications, Orange, Va.

Boston & Sandwich / New England Glass

A Collectors Handbook of Blown and Pressed American Glass, Richard Carter Barret, The Bennington Museum Bennington, Vt. 05201

Boston & Sandwich Glass Co. Catalog year 1874, Lee Publications, Wellesley Hills, Mass.

The Sandwich Glass Museum Collection Sandwich Glass Museum Sandwich, Mass.

Cambridge

The Cambridge Glass Co. 1930-1934, National Cambridge Collectors, Inc. Collector books, P.O. Box 3009 Paducah, Ky. 42001 or National Cambridge Collectors, Inc. P.O. Box 416 Cambridge, Ohio 43725

The Cambridge Glass Book, Harold & Judy Bennett, 506 South 9th Street, Cambridge, Ohio 43725

The Cambridge Glass Co. a reprint of parts of old company catalogs, Mary, Lyle, and Lynn Welker 2 East Main Street New Concord, Ohio 43762

1903 catalog of Pressed and Blown Glass Ware, the Cambridge Glass Co. Harold & Judy Bennett

Duncan-Miller

The Encyclopedia of Duncan Glass, Gail Krouse Exposition Press, Inc., 900 South Oyster Bay Road Hicksville, N.Y. 11801

The Book of Duncan Glass, Frances Bones, Wallace-Homestead Co. Des Moines, Iowa 50305

Fenton

Fenton Glass The First Twenty-Five Years, William Heacock, O-Val Advertising Corp., P.O. Box 663, Marietta, Ohio 45750

Fenton Glass The Second Twenty-Five Years, William Heacock

Fostoria

Fostoria - Its First Fifty Years, Hazel Marie Weatherman, 4501 Jackson Drive, Rt. 12 Springfield, Mo. 65804

Heisey

Three major company sales catalog re-prints: *Heisey's Glassware for the Table* (years 1937-1938) *Heisey's Glassware* - pressed ware catalog No. 109 (years 1929-1930) *Heisey Glassware* - catalog No. 75 (dated 1913).

Published by P-W Publications copies may be obtained from:
Collector Books P.O. Box 3009 Paducah Ky. 42001 or Heisey Collectors of America, Inc. P.O. Box 27 Newark, Ohio 43055.

Heisey - by Imperial, Newark Heisey Collectors Club, Published by: Heisey Collectors of America, Inc. P.O. Box 27 Newark, Ohio 43055

Heisey Glass - In Color, Virginia & Loren Yeakley, 640 Melanie Court Newark, Ohio 43055

Heisey Glass - In Color Book 1, Virginia & Loaren Yeakley

Heisey Glassware, Viola N. Cudd, The Antique Barn Route 1, Box 11 Brenham, Texas 77833

We do not have a title or release date, but it is expected that members of the Heisey Collectors of America, Inc. will release a new publication on Heisey candlesticks in the summer or fall of 1982. This book will be a *must* for anyone who collects glass candlesticks.

Imperial

Imperial Glass, Margaret & Douglas Archer, Collector Books P.O. Box 3009 Paducah, Ky. 42001 or Douglas Archer P.O. Box 919 Kernersville N.C. 27284

Candlewick The Jewel of Imperial, Mary M. Wetzel, P.O. Box 594 Notre Dame, Ind. 46556

Imperial Glass, Richard & Wilma Ross, 565 West 41st street Shadyside, Ohio 43947 Published by: Wallace-Homestead Book Co. Des Moines, Iowa 50305

McKee

The Complete Book of McKee Glass, Sandra McPhee Stout, Trojan Press 310 East 18th Avenue North Kansas City, Mo. 64116

New Martinsville

The New Martinsville Glass Story, Everett R. & Addie R. Miller, 8700 Lansing Avenue, Rives Junction, Mich. 49277

The New Martinsville Glass Story - Book II, Everett R. & Addie R. Miller

Paden City

Paden City - The Color Company, Jerry Barnett, P.O. Box 949 Cambridge, Ohio 43725

Pairpoint

Pairpoint Glass, Leonard E. Padgett, 9308 Branywine Road Clinton, Md. 20735 Published by: Wallace-Homestead Book Co. Des Moines, Iowa 50305

Sinclaire

H. P. Sinclaire, Jr., Glass Maker Volume 1 & 2, Estelle Sinclaire, Farrar Farrar Books P.O. Box 2029 Garden City, N.Y. 11530

Steuben

The Glass of Frederick Carder, Paul V. Gardner, Crown Publishers, Inc. New York

U.S. Glass Co.

Tiffin Glassmasters, Fred Bickenheuser, Glassmasters Publications P.O. Box 524 Grove City, Ohio 43123

Tiffin Glassmasters - Book II, Fred Bickenheuser

Societies

In addition to the publications listed, much knowledge of the collecting of glass can be obtained from collectors clubs, societies, local and National organizations. We can by no means list local organizations, but we will list some of the major organizations that we have address for:

National Cambridge Collectors, Inc.
P.O. Box 416, Cambridge, Ohio 43725

National Depression Glass Association, Inc.
8337 Santa Fe Lane, Shawnee Mission, Ks. 66212

Fenton Art Glass Collectors of America, Inc.
P.O. Box 2441, Appleton, Wi. 54913

Fostoria Glass Society of America, Inc.
P.O. Box 826 Moundsville, W. Va. 26041

Heisey Collectors of America, Inc.
P.O. Box 27, Newark, Ohio 43055

The Imperial Glass Collectors Society
P.O. Box 4012, Silver Spring, Md. 20904